NORTH CAROLINA
STATE BOARD OF COMMUNITY COLLEGES
WAKE TECHNICAL COMMUNITY COLLEGE

WITHDRAWN

The Romance of Innocence and The Myth of History

National Association of Baptist Professors of Religion

JOURNAL

Perspectives in Religious Studies
Editor: Watson E. Mills
 Mercer University

SERIES

Special Studies Series
Editor: Edgar McKnight
 Furman University

Dissertation Series
Editor: James Wm. McClendon
 Church Divinity School
 of the Pacific

Bibliographic Series
Editor: David M. Scholer
 North Park College
 and Theological Seminary

THE ROMANCE OF INNOCENCE AND THE MYTH OF HISTORY

Faulkner's Religious Critique
of Southern Culture

NABPR Dissertation Series, Number 7

---

by
John Sykes

MP MERCER UNIVERSITY PRESS, Macon, Georgia 31207

ISBN 0-86554-354-2

Copyright © 1989
Mercer University Press
Macon, Georgia 31207
All rights reserved
Printed in the United States of America.

The paper used in this publication meets the minimum requirements
of American National Standard for Information Sciences—Permanence
of Paper for Printed Library Materials, ANSI Z39.48-1984. ∞

Library of Congress Cataloging-in-Publication Data
Sykes, John, 1952–
 The romance of innocence and the myth of history : Faulkner's religious critique of southern culture / by John Sykes.
  p. 128—(NABPR dissertation series ; no. 7)
  Includes bibliographical references.
  ISBN 0-86554-354-2 (alk. paper)
  1. Faulkner, William, 1897-1962—Criticism and interpretation.
2. Faulkner, William, 1897-1962—Religion. 3. Southern States in literature. 4. Religion in literature. 5. History in literature.
6. Myth in literature. 7. Innocence (Psychology) in literature.
I. Title.   II. Series.
PS3511.A86Z9746   1989
813'.52—dc20   89-9437
                                                            CIP

TABLE OF CONTENTS

INTRODUCTION   1

CHAPTER 1
Failure of the Feminine Ideal
and Cultural Crisis: *The Sound and the Fury*   13

CHAPTER 2
Rejection of the Male Ideal and the Burden
of History: *Absalom, Absalom!*   33

CHAPTER 3
A Puritan Indictment: Myth vs. Irony
in *Light in August*   55

CHAPTER 4
The Ironic Myth: *Go Down, Moses*   85

CONCLUSION   103

For Cornelia Boone Gupton
who not only endured,
but rejoiced

INTRODUCTION

While the particular purpose of this study is to provide a unified interpretation of the religious dimension of Faulkner's greatest fiction, the larger perspective from which I have treated his work is that of the crisis of historicism. By "historicism" I mean the jolt supplied by the work of such thinkers as Vico, Hume, Nietzsche, and D.F. Strauss to what is commonly called foundational thinking.[1] Faulkner, no less than these men, is conscious of the religious loss incurred with the discovery that culture is not a "mirror of nature" but a temporary human edifice. By virtue of his recognition that Southern society was based on a false myth which sought to deny history, Faulkner was led to doubt the efficacy of any myth which seeks to give history human significance.

Faulkner's exploration of the Southern mind convinced him that the human capacity for self-delusion is so great as to make questionable the possibility of any kind of genuine knowledge. Yet "reality" seemed to him so bleak as to necessitate the comfort of illusions; history stripped of myth was simply intolerable.

Indeed, Faulkner comes to see the Southern crisis as a microcosm of the larger problematic of modern culture as a whole. For him, Western man stands in the twilight of the idols which Nietzsche had foreseen. Like Nietzsche, Faulkner feels the need to reclaim myth in the face of history; they both realize that to do so requires a new, self-conscious attitude toward myth, what Ricoeur speaks of as a second naiveté.[2] But whereas Nietzsche believes that myth may become a kind of supreme fiction which the *Übermensch* joyfully

---

[1] See Richard Rorty, *Philosophy and the Mirror of Nature* (Princeton: Princeton University Press, 1979) and Jeffrey Stout, *The Flight From Authority* (Notre Dame: Notre Dame Press, 1981).

[2] "The Hermeneutics of Symbols and Philosophical Reflection," trans. Denis Savage, *International Philosophical Quarterly* 2 (1962), 191–218.

embraces as the expression of his own vitality, Faulkner clings to the hope that ironic myth—myth, that is, which is held *as* myth—may indeed provide access to ultimate reality. Faulkner holds out for the possibility of a new basis for meaning that is not a mere human projection. He attempts to create a myth which is aware of the relativizing force of history, yet which points beyond itself in a gesture of hope.

For Nietzsche, historical consciousness leads to the conclusion that God is dead. For Faulkner, it is a sign of profound alienation from "a God . . . who rests in the now."[3] Unlike Nietzsche, Faulkner resisted the belief that the door to what Fredric Jameson has called the "prison-house of language"[4] is locked from the outside, and that the essence of man is "the will to power."[5] His art is an attempt to make human life religiously meaningful again by depicting it as nobly tragic. The will to power cannot be denied, but in the Yoknapatawpha novels it can be checked by the desire for communion. While in Faulkner's world consciousness itself alienates man from the sources of life, he is nonetheless granted intimations of immortality which inspire hope where there is courage. For Faulkner God is that dynamic flow of Being which no myth may ever capture but which the ravages of history cannot destroy. This God is a possibility never realized by man—a possibility which may in fact be an illusion. But if illusion it be, it remains the only dream worth dreaming, the lone alternative to despair.

Like his fellow survivor of a lost traditional culture Mircea Eliade, Faulkner knew that the destruction of myth provokes religious crisis. "History" in its modern sense threatens to destroy "cosmos" altogether. By fashioning a cosmos of his own Faulkner hoped to cultivate through art a religious sensibility that would be immune to the vicissitudes of history. He remained sceptical, however, that art could provide the unqualified religious affirmation which "innocent" myth had once afforded. He thus became a prophet of "the almost meaningful"[6] whose religious vision took the form of an ironic myth.

By placing Faulkner in the context of historicism I have adopted the new frame in which Richard King has placed the entire Southern Renaissance. It has become a commonplace among critics of the Southern Renaissance that the intellectual awakening which began to bear fruit in the 1920's was oc-

---

[3]Interview with Loic Bouvard in *Lion in the Garden,* James B. Meriwether and Michael Millgate, eds. (Lincoln: University of Nebraska Press, 1980) 70.

[4]*The Prison-House of Language: A Critical Account of Structuralism and Russian Formalism* (Princeton: Princeton University Press, 1972).

[5]See Nietzsche's development of the idea of the will to power in *On the Genealogy of Morals* in *On the Genealogy of Morals and Ecce Homo,* Walter Kaufmann, tr. (New York: Vintage Books, 1967).

[6]John Irwin, *Doubling and Incest, Repetiton and Revenge* (Baltimore: The Johns Hopkins Press, 1975), 9.

casioned by a general cultural crisis which Southern intellectuals had already discerned.[7] The ravages of the Civil War and Reconstruction had effectively destroyed the old planter-dominated society, while simultaneously calling forth a nostalgic mythologizing of the old order. By the 1920's the war and its immediate consequences were a full generation behind, and the new group of artists and thinkers who were growing to maturity had both the perspective of distance and the broadening experience of the First World War to help them comprehend the cultural crisis provoked by the death of a traditional society.

Such writers as John Crowe Ransom, Allen Tate, and Robert Penn Warren had at once a sense of the living reality of the traditional culture of the Old South, and of the passing away of the *ancien regime.* And in the ironic and complex syntax of the Fugitives' poetry we can see sophisticated minds trying to make sense of a revered tradition which is disintegrating under the pressures of modernity.[8]

The commonly accepted interpretation of these writers is that they were particularly well equipped to defend traditional values in the midst of the general crisis of modern sensibility. As Southerners, they possessed

> a cast of mind which suspected abstraction and utopian schemes, was fundamentally religious, and had a sense of life's tragic conflicts, and which was firmly rooted in place and community. This Southern mentality had arisen from the region's experience of occupation and defeat, poverty, and of racial oppression and guilt. The result was an ironic view of the overweening ambitions and dangerous innocence of those who would change society and human nature. Unlike most Americans, Southerners allegedly possessed an active sense of history and historical consciousness.[9]

According to this assessment, which King has called the "Tate-Woodward-Brooks" thesis, the Southern Renaissance was an essentially conservative movement which sought to preserve the cultural achievements of the old order in the face of the modern challenge.

The work of William Faulkner has generally been identified with this larger intellectual movement, and with justification. But his Yoknapatawpha fiction compels one to make two important qualifications (one of them evident in the best recent commentary on Faulkner, and the other not yet forcefully stated) of this frequently taken approach to his work. The first is that Faulkner was more critical of the South than this essentially Agrarian interpretation of him

---

[7]The classic statement of this view is that of Allen Tate, "The Profession of Letters in the South," in *Essays of Four Decades* (Chicago: Swallow Press, 1968).

[8]The best sustained treatment of the Fugitives is that of John L. Stewart, *The Burden of Time* (Princeton: University of Princeton Press, 1965).

[9]Richard King, "Framework of a Renaissance" in *Faulkner and the Southern Renaissance,* Fowler and Abadie, eds. (Jackson: University of Mississippi Press, 1981), 14–15. See also C. Vann Woodward, "Why the Southern Renaissance?" in *The Virginia Quarterly Review,* 51:2 (Spring, 1975), 227–39.

would admit.[10] As the recent work of such critics as Richard King, John Irwin, and David Minter makes clear, Faulkner was not, as Cleanth Brooks would have it, opposing the Southern tradition at its best to the abstracted, rootless, and Godless ethos of modernity. Instead, Faulkner was making a scathing indictment of a culture which had cloaked its origins and disguised its sins in the garb of a false romance. The South as seen through Faulkner's fiction is a society which has sought to evade history. Far from possessing the historical consciousness which other Americans lack, Southerners have so mythicized their past as to be no longer capable of assuming responsibility for their history. Faulkner's genius lies precisely in his ability to break free of the Southern romance of innocence into a conscious acceptance of history.

As King has forcefully argued, then, the major writers of the Southern Renaissance are distinguished by their sense of their own culture's transiency: the destruction of the old order engendered in them a sharp sense of the impermanence of every cultural edifice.[11] In Faulkner this loss of all illusions resulted in the view of history which Hayden White denominates the ironic.[12] He did not, in other words, want to extol the virtues of the Old South but wanted rather to call them radically into question from the perspective of an ironic historical consciousness.

A second qualification of the "Tate-Woodward-Brooks thesis" as it applies to Faulkner is one which King himself does not provide—namely that Faulkner's critique of the South is a religious critique.[13] Faulkner is not upholding the fundamentally religious sensibility of his region in the face of an increasingly secularized Western culture; he is exposing the perversity of a religious understanding which has in fact alienated the South from nature and history. Southern religion has sponsored the state of estrangement which the South unknowingly shares with its parent culture. What Faulkner calls "Puritanism" is precisely the mistaken religious self-understanding which has left the South vulnerable to the dissociation of sensibility which characterizes modern secularized society at large. As Allen Tate correctly discerns, the South's religious vision is its greatest liability rather than its best defense against abstraction and rootlessness.[14]

In the South which Faulkner brings to life in his fiction, religion is a powerful force for self-deception. It is one of the primary elements in that romance of innocence by which the South avoids facing the truth about itself.

---

[10]King, "Framework of a Renaissance," 14.
[11]Richard King, *A Southern Renaissance* (New York: Oxford University Press, 1980), 65ff.
[12]*Metahistory* (Baltimore: The Johns Hopkins Press, 1973), 37.
[13]*Cf.* King, *A Southern Renaissance*, 7. King dismisses the notion that the writers of the Southern Renaissance had religious concerns without arguing his case.
[14]"Remarks on the Southern Religion" in *I'll Take My Stand* (New York: Harper & Brothers, 1930).

Like that curious character in *Light in August,* Gail Hightower, the South has blended Puritanism with the myth of the Cavalier in order to disguise the raw will to power which has erected a second-hand civilization through a cruel system of exploitation. And one of Faulkner's principal concerns is to expose the self-deluding nature of Puritanism.

But Faulkner's work is religious in a deeper sense as well. He is aware that to undermine the legitimating religious framework of his society is to endanger what Peter Berger calls its "plausibility structure."[15] Faulkner seeks not only to unmask the perverse face of Southern religion, but to discover through art an alternative religious vision which will answer the threat of *anomie*. As the following chapters will show, Faulkner considers Puritanism to have created an unbridgeable gap between man and the natural world. There is a sustained longing in his work for what we might call a new sacramentalism. He hopes to find a means whereby man's history is annulled through its connection with the timeless patterns of the natural cycle and the divine spirit of life that is present in them.

Sprinkled throughout Faulkner's fiction are hierophantic moments in which man is put briefly in touch with the divine through an unmediated experience of the natural world. Perhaps the clearest examples of such moments are to be found in *Go Down, Moses* when Ike encounters the great stag and Old Ben, but similar occasions are to be found in Dilsey's Easter morning ecstasy and Joe Christmas's nocturnal walk through the Burden farm on the night before he kills Joanna. In each of these moments Faulkner's characters are removed from the rush of human history and placed amidst the timeless rhythms of nature. Consciousness no longer places a barrier between them and the life that surrounds them; they achieve a kind of beatific vision. What makes Faulkner's fiction problematical is that he attempts to establish through art the mystic communion which must come to these characters as an unmediated experience. In what he senses to be a hopeless endeavor, Faulkner the novelist strives to bridge the gap between man and nature which, according to his own assessment, willful consciousness can only broaden.

Though he never fully achieves it, Faulkner strains toward a religious vision which will reverse man's fall into consciousness and history. In what I shall call the mythic mode of his art, he seeks to recreate the cyclical, volitionless world which he identifies with the fauns, satyrs, and goddesses of Greek myth. But for Faulkner, mythic consciousness is a strategy for escaping history, not a means of recovering it. Faulkner never wins through to a full-fledged religious affirmation which can take the place of the Puritanism which he criticizes, because for him myth cannot accommodate history.

---

[15]Peter Berger, *The Sacred Canopy* (Garden City, NY: Anchor Books, 1969), 45.

Faulkner is painfully aware of the fact that myth in the hands of the artist becomes the tool of an imagination which aims above all else to please itself. Unlike the ancient Greek for whom myth was an expression of faith and an accurate picture of reality, for Faulkner myth is wish-fulfillment, a consciously fabricated illusion. As Gerald Graff has said of Northrop Frye's work, in Faulkner myth creates "the order of things as they should be as projected by human purpose and 'desire' . . . "[16] History stands over against myth in Faulkner's work as reality to illusion, yet the historical as such is meaningless. History divorced from myth is devoid of those patterns which would make it comprehensible and value-laden; it can be "nothing but a theater of dehumanization, a place of bondage and torture."[17]

By stripping the South of its false myth (the romance of innocence), Faulkner has left history chaotic and unformed. The conflicting and fragmented narratives which make up *Absalom, Absalom!* and *The Sound and the Fury* are testimony to the spiritual crisis which results when there is no myth available wherewith to give shape and meaning to history.[18] In Faulkner's great fiction, myth and history are at loggerheads. Faulkner uses an ironic sense of the historical to explode the myth by which the South understands itself. Then, sensing the despair to which a completely demythologized history leads, he creates his own myths which, however, he knows to be artful illusions.[19] Art thus becomes first a method of entering history, but finally a means of escape from its chaos.

It is only at the end of his most creative period that Faulkner is able to bring myth and history into reciprocal relation by means of an ironic myth which conceives of the self-conscious attempt to mythologize history as necessary but finally doomed to futility. He comes to believe that while man is inherently alienated from the source of being, he is nonetheless part of a larger, ordered whole. This larger spiritual reality is all but inaccessible to conscious man, and the brief glimpses he has of it are always subject to doubt. Yet to live out one's life by faith in this holy reality is the highest end of man. This religious conviction allows him to move from the borders of nihilism to a tragic view of the human condition.

---

[16]*Literature Against Itself: Literary Ideas in Modern Society* (Chicago: University of Chicago Press, 1979), 182.

[17]Frank Lentricchia, *After the New Criticism* (Chicago: University of Chicago Press, 1980), 26.

[18]Mircea Eliade has described this general crisis from the standpoint of the history of religion in *The Myth of the Eternal Return or, Cosmos and History,* Willard Trask, tr. (Princeton: Princeton University Press, 1954).

[19]I am not using "demythologize" in the way which Rudolf Bultmann employs the term, but in the literal sense of removing myth. On the difference between demythologizing and "demystification" see Paul Ricoeur, *Freud and Philosophy: An Essay on Interpretation,* Denis Savage, trans. (New Haven: Yale University Press, 1970).

In employing the terms "myth" and "history" to discuss Faulkner's religious vision I am following the lead of Lewis Simpson.[20] For Simpson, these categories are basic to any thorough understanding of the crisis which has manifested itself in the literature of the modern period. While I am indebted to him at many points, I have sought to use the twin notions of myth and history with a precision which Simpson's work lacks. As is true of any concept which gains wide scholarly currency, these terms have come to take on a wide range of meaning in our period. One needs only to mention the names of Mircea Eliade, Rudolf Bultmann, Paul Ricoeur, Ernst Cassirer, and Northrop Frye to recall that the concept of myth has loomed large in recent humanistic humanistic scholarship. The discovery of the historical nature of human existence, which is usually credited to Giambattista Vico, has been the starting point for thinkers as diverse as G.W.F. Hegel, Friedrich Nietzsche, Ernst Troeltsch, D.F. Strauss, R.G. Collingwood, Martin Heidegger, and Michel Foucault. It is not within the scope of my present project to enter the debate that these giants of the modern era have conducted. My own understanding of the relation between myth and history owes most to Eliade's work *Cosmos and History,* and to Frye's use of myth in his literary criticism. I am also indebted to Nietzsche's *The Use and Abuse of History* as interpreted by Hayden White and Richard King.

By "myth" I mean primarily a type of story which is believed to have "some exceptional significance in explaining [essential] features of life. . . . "[21] While myths in their original setting may be taken as literally true, they aim at truth in the deeper sense of "an analogical imaging forth of the eminent reality of [their divine] ground."[22] In myth, time is annulled in favor of the eternal.[23] Thus myth has as one of its functions the interpretation of ultimate reality; it stands as a kind of symbolic metaphysics. When this "symbolic instrument" is "sacralized," it becomes religious myth.[24] Indeed, the deepest purpose of myth is to create for human consciousness a cos-

---

[20]*The Brazen Face of History* (Baton Rouge: LSU Press, 1980).

[21]Northrup Frye, *Fables of Identity: Studies in Poetic Mythology* (New York: Harcourt Brace Jovanovich, 1963), 30.

[22]Eliade, ix.

[23]Eugene Webb, *Eric Voegelin: Philosopher of History* (Seattle, WA: University of Washington Press, 1981), 145.

[24]Jacques Waardenburg has written a perceptive assessment of recent treatments of myth in "Symbolic Aspects of Myth," *Myth, Symbol, and Reality,* Alan M. Olson, ed. (Notre Dame: University of Notre Dame Press, 1980), 41–68. According to Waardenburg, myth always has as its function the construal of ultimate reality (58). Myth becomes religious when the "symbolic instrument" which creates a certain understanding of reality "becomes sacralized and consequently absolutized" (57). While myth is not inherently religious, it is inclined toward the religious, so to speak. Waardenburg seems to believe, as I contend, that myth is a necessary precondition for religion.

mos out of the chaos of uninterpreted experience. Without myth (thus broadly understood) there is no human access to the divine.

But myth also serves a social function. Every society seeks to legitimate its own structure by identifying it with that of ultimate reality itself. This process is what Peter Berger calls "the cosmization of the nomos."[25] At yet another level, myth functions as art. In Frye's sense of *mythoi,* myths operate as basic plot forms which control all narrative discourse.[26] Disjointed myths may continue to function as art even when deprived of their religious, metaphysical, and social functions.

History, by contrast, is the realm of actual events in time; at its most basic level it is what Hayden White has called the "historical field," the raw data of "what happened." Since the Enlightenment, there has been a growing conviction that human reality is restricted to the historical sphere. The notion of eternity, the world *in illo tempore* which myth seeks to invoke, has increasingly appeared to be an illusion. Whereas the presupposition of myth is that time is real only to the extent that in it eternal cycles are endlessly repeated, the assumption of historical consciousness is that eternity is a human projection which seeks to deny the reality of time.

As Mircea Eliade has eloquently argued, the displacement of myth by history is fraught with spiritual dangers. What Eliade calls "the terror of history" is the fear that events have no meaning or purpose beyond themselves.[27] The loss of the world of myth removes the ordered cosmos which allows man to find meaning in the face of death and suffering. Without some alternative narrative pattern to serve the ordering function which myth once supplied, history becomes an indifferent tide which overwhelms every human attempt to construct a "cosmos." It is this general sense of time as divorced from eternity and of event as devoid of human meaning which, following Eliade, I have assigned to the term history.

The modern crisis may be seen as precisely the need to restore time to a framework in which it has metahistorical significance; that is, to forge a myth *of* history. Hayden White's *Metahistory* can be read as a study of the way in which philosophies of history have, since the Enlightenment, taken over the mythic function of ordering time. It is no coincidence that, in identifying the modes of emplotment which serve as the paradigms of the great nineteenth-century historians, White has adopted the scheme of archetypes which Northrop Frye derives from ancient myth. Nor is it surprising that several of the great figures whom White examines (most notably, Hegel) show a marked tendency to sacralize the myth of history which their work embodies. In

---

[25]Berger, 24.
[26]Frye, 24.
[27]Eliade, 151.

White's view the construction of an historical account from the raw data of the historical field is always an act of *poiesis* rather than *mimesis,* and thus in the deepest sense of the term, it is a kind of myth.

In this study I will chart Faulkner's religious project from his attempt to "indict" and "escape" the South in *The Sound and the Fury* to the ironic myth he fashions in *Go Down, Moses.* I will show how in Faulkner's first great novel he is at once indicting the myth which I call the Southern romance of innocence and "escaping" from it into the self-conscious mythic wholeness of art. The second of these twin aims is imperfectly realized, however, because the Christian myth to which Faulkner turns at the end of the novel remains, in his treatment of it, an entirely aesthetic configuration which fails to redeem the bleak reality of history. The aspect of the Southern myth which Faulkner here attacks is that of the white virgin, who is the symbol of virtue in the romance of innocence. The "failure" of the novel, which Faulkner often noted, is the inability of the Compson brothers and the omniscient narrator to replace the symbol of virtue which Caddy's undeniable promiscuous sexuality has effectively destroyed. As is the case throughout Faulkner's fiction, sexuality is here the sign of man's emergence from myth into history.

From Faulkner's indictment of the Southern feminine ideal in *The Sound and the Fury* I will move to his reexamination of the myth of the founder in *Absalom, Absalom!.* Here Faulkner turns his full attention to the Southern past as it is captured in the fragmented narratives woven around the figure of Thomas Sutpen. Sutpen emerges as the true type of the Southern planter because he is completely absorbed by the romance of innocence with which his society has masked the naked will to power. In Henry's rejection of father and brother and Miss Rosa's outrage over Sutpen's ruthlessness, we feel the stirring of an internal religious revolt against the hegemony of the romance of innocence. To the extent that it demands obedience to divine law as a check to human pride, what Faulkner calls Puritanism stands over against the Cavalier tradition which Sutpen appropriates. "Coldfield morality" serves as the instrument of ethical negation in *Absalom, Absalom!,* but it cannot provide the religious affirmation necessary for a redemptive alternative to the will to power.

The inefficacy of the Puritan tradition is exposed in *Light in August,* where Faulkner scrutinizes Yoknapatawpha's explicitly religious consciousness. In this novel we see the way in which the Cavalier and Puritan traditions actually cooperate in the romance of innocence. The Puritan substitutes Election for aristocratic privilege as his charter for self-aggrandizement, but in both traditions the world is seen as a neutral field where the individual will must carry out its design. The divorce of will from the world leads to obsession and fantasy, which all of the Puritans in *Light in August* display. Gail Hightower, that curious combination of Presbyterian preacher and Civil War romanticist, is Faulkner's chief vehicle for exploring the union of Puritan and Cavalier in the romance of innocence.

Joe Christmas, who is one of Faulkner's virtually mute figures, is at once the victim and the saint of Puritanism. He is locked entirely within the false mythic framework of Calvinistic religion, and his "crucifixion" brings to logical culminaton the religion of death to which he, like his executioners, finally subscribes. Hightower, who is the most enlightened character in the novel, is completely ineffectual in his attempt to prevent Joe's tragedy, and the state of fantasy into which at last he completely lapses is his retreat from the terror of history.

The only alternative in the novel to the religion of death which claims Joe Christmas is to be found in the pastoral reverie that surrounds Lena Grove. Here again, Faulkner seeks to escape history through an alternative myth which denies history. Byron Bunch's comic pursuit of this Southern earth goddess in no sense redeems the death of Christmas; instead, it offers an aesthetic image of mythic wholeness which ignores the dark reality of human consciousness sundered from nature.

Faulkner brings his own myth to bear on history in *Go Down, Moses*. Ike McCaslin is the first of Faulkner's characters to possess both historical consciousness and a vision of man in harmony with nature. The hunt story contained within "The Bear" describes an Edenic existence which Ike uses as the basis for evaluating the society for which he feels he has inherited responsibility. He rejects his patrimony on the grounds that man does not own the earth but only shares in its life. In the grim record of his forefathers' dealings with their slaves and tenants he sees a kind of proof that the property relation produces exploitation. And thus he refuses to accept the plantation he has inherited, since to do so would be to continue the pattern of exploitation and to break that communion with the spirit of nature into which Sam Fathers has initiated him in the big woods.

From Faulkner's perspective, however, Ike misreads the lessons of Eden. The story of the killing of Old Ben is in fact a parable which discloses the inescapability of history and the will to power. Even in the big woods man lives by slaughter. Consciousness itself alienates man from nature. The kind of reconciliation that Ike desires is impossible because it would require the annihilation of will. Ike's idealistic gestures are possible only for one who has withdrawn to the periphery of history. As Ike is a mere observer in the ritual slaying of the god of the wood in the hunt story, so he lives on the fringe of the world of farms and banks. In Faulkner's view, the price of culture is alienation; the continuance of society requires the violation of nature. So Ike's refusal to exercise the will to power simply removes him from the life of his society, and thus it is no accident that he remains childless.

ROMANCE OF INNOCENCE/MYTH OF HISTORY

The myth which Ike whole-heartedly embraces becomes in Faulkner's treatment of it an ironic myth of history. It is mythic in the sense that it posits an explanation of the human condition, but it is ironic in that it discloses the inescapability of history. The point of Faulkner's myth is that human society is *not* the reflection of a timeless natural order; alienation from nature is what makes human culture possible. Culture is the creation of consciousness, and consciousness brings with it the will to power. Human existence is tragic because consciousness dooms man to separation and isolation. While Faulkner clings to the hope that the spirit of nature to which Ike dedicates himself does indeed hover at the periphery of human life, it is actually available only through the private vision of those poetic souls who are able to use consciousness against itself to achieve a second naiveté.

For Faulkner, every truly moral intention is pegged on the hope that human history is not entirely self-enclosed. The ironic myth is meant to open a window in the prison of consciousness so that it becomes possible to glimpse Being. Those epiphanies of mythic meaning which inspire the man of conscience may indeed be illusions; the will to power is so deeply engrained in human society that no act of conscience can root it out. But the inevitably tragic effort of the courageous individual to bring moral order to the chaos of history is from Faulkner's perspective the splendid failure which prevents the human enterprise from becoming a grim absurdity. Faulkner's ironic myth is thus an attempt to make history meaningful without denying its terror. The only myth which can tolerate the light of history is an ironic one; religious affirmation is at best a possibility which can never be fully realized. In Faulkner's tragic vision, man must be content with the almost meaningful.

CHAPTER 1

FAILURE OF THE FEMININE IDEAL AND CULTURAL CRISIS: *THE SOUND AND THE FURY*

I

From the beginning, critics have debated the role of history in *The Sound and the Fury* and *Absalom, Absalom!*. Influential Southern critics such as Cleanth Brooks, Louis Rubin, and C. Vann Woodward have seen in these works an opposition between the values of an enlightened Southerner who represents the best of his tradition and the evils of a naive modernism. Non-Southerners, among them Irving Howe, Michael Millgate, and Alfred Kazin, have been more interested in pointing out the ways in which Faulkner is critical of the South. Howe, for example, treats *Absalom, Absalom!* as a novel about the "fall of the homeland" and Sutpen as a representative Southern planter.[1] Brooks insists that Sutpen's flaw lies precisely in his naive and rationalistic misunderstanding of the role which he usurps.[2] The irony here is that the best interpreters of Faulkner from his own region have been least

---

[1] *William Faulkner: A Critical Study,* (Chicago: University of Chicago Press, third edition, 1975), 24.
[2] *The Yoknapatawpha Country,* (New Haven: Yale University Press, 1963; paper repr. 1976), .295ff. Brooks has also devoted an entire appendix to refuting the claim that *Absalom, Absalom!* is in any sense a revisionist reading of Southern history in *Toward Yoknapatawpha and Beyond* (New Haven: Yale University Press, 1978), 283–300.

willing to examine the image of the South that his works project. In the striking case of Brooks's reading of *Absalom, Absalom!*, one of the finest critics of his generation defends the implausible view that the novel in which Faulkner most explicitly treats the origins of the South is focused on a character who is in no way representative of Southern culture.

A version of the same critical controversy has surrounded *The Sound and the Fury*. The novel has in some instances been read as depicting the demise of the Southern aristocratic class and in others as rendering a psychological drama in which regional factors are incidental.[3] Critics have relied heavily on the example of Quentin Compson in both interpretations. Quentin clearly sees himself as upholding an aristocratic code of honor; yet his obsession with Caddy's virginity seems to be part of a private neurosis which bears no general significance for his society.

Recent critical work has embraced a more inclusive view of Faulkner which reconciles these conflicting interpretations of his work. In the best current commentaries he is thought of as having been indeed sensitive to the loss of tradition and distressed by the rootlessness and alienation which characterize modernity, but as having found no haven in the values of his own regional culture. Instead, he is seen as having been keenly aware that the mind of the South suffered from an internal crisis. Essays by such critics as Richard King, John Irwin, and David Minter have shown that Faulkner was not, as Brooks would have it, opposing the Southern tradition at its best to the abstracted, rootless, and godless ethos of modernity. Far from upholding the values of a tradition which modern rationalized man had forsaken, Faulkner is conceived as having wanted to expose the emptiness of a tradition which had driven its heirs into a state of deep alienation. In short, his critique of modernity is on this view thought to begin with his indictment of the South.

Lewis Simpson has provided the framework in which Faulkner's understanding of the modern situation may be seen in its entirety. He considers Faulkner's work to be characterized by a dialectic between myth and history.[4] History, in Simpson's sense, is an undetermined and linear sequence of events whose only meaning is that which human consciousness assigns it. Myth, by contrast, is the narrative attempt to annul time; myths are stories which endeavor to place human activity in the preexistent patterns of the natural order and thus to stamp culture with the seal of eternity. History threatens to strip time of meaning on the one hand, and myth seeks to deny time on the other.

---

[3]*Vide* Michael Millgate, *The Achievement of William Faulkner* (Lincoln: University of Nebraska Press, 1978), 97, and Andre Bleikasten, *The Most Splendid Failure: Faulkner's "The Sound and the Fury"* (Bloomington: Indiana University Press, 1976).

[4]*The Brazen Face of History* (Baton Rouge: LSU Press, 1980).

As Richard King has shown, Faulkner saw the cultural edifice of the South as a mythic construct which sought to evade history.[5] The South was deluded by its romance of innocence, which claimed that Southern social structures were a continuation of those of pre-industrialized European culture. In giving the lie to this myth, Faulkner was conscious that its destruction created a moral vacuum. He seeks, therefore, to fashion a new myth through art in order to supply the imagination with the order lacking in history itself. Faulkner's ultimate hope, partially realized in *Go Down, Moses,* is to discover a myth which will reclaim history, but in the bulk of his great fiction the relation between myth and history is simply antithetical.

Faulkner's symbol of the fall from myth into history is sexuality, which in his view at once reveals man's estrangement from nature and his desperate desire for reunion with "the other." Even in his early poetry, the fall into sexuality is attended by the loss of the mythic world of fauns and nymphs and by the appearance of historical consciousness in the guise of Satan.[6] John Irwin, who has presented the most thorough of recent readings of Quentin Compson, demonstrates that the themes of sex and history are also inextricably linked in Faulkner's most complex character.[7]

The insight that Faulkner's work springs from the dialectic of myth and history thus allows us to unify previous interpretations of the Yoknapatawpha fiction which seemed to conflict. Faulkner's novels are not "historical fiction" in the common sense of the term, but they are deeply concerned with the nature of history. *The Sound and the Fury* describes both the demise of the Southern aristocracy and the psychological drama of a family warped by neuroses. In Faulkner's view the myth which legitimates Southern society denies history by denying sexuality. Since sex and history are necessarily connected, it is inevitable that such a myth should produce a neurotic understanding of sexuality. Thus the Compsons' psychological maladies and their social position are inseparable; the Compsons' inability to confront Caddy's sexuality is a revelation of their failure to accommodate history. The crisis in Southern culture is, in Faulkner's reading of it, the result of a psycho-sexual drama.

The unifying interpretation of Faulkner which I hope to bring to focus in the following chapters will illustrate the ways in which Faulkner's project in the Yoknapatawpha fiction is a religious enterprise. As Mircea Eliade has

---

[5] *Vide* Richard King, "Framework of a Renaissance" in *Faulkner and the Southern Renaissance* (Jackson: University of Mississippi Press, 1981), 3–21 and *A Southern Renaissance: The Cultural Awakening of the South, 1930–1955* (Oxford: Oxford University Press, 1980).

[6] Simpson, 187ff.

[7] *Doubling and Incest, Repetition and Revenge* (Baltimore: Johns Hopkins Press, 1975; paper repr. 1980).

clearly seen, the loss of myth provokes what is fundamentally a religious crisis.[8] Faulkner's urge to replace the myth which he has helped to destroy discloses a desire to find some new means of access to the powers which shape human existence. Once stripped of all his myths, man becomes the victim of history; the flow of events which he plainly does not control sweeps him away to no purpose. Human suffering, inevitable in any case, becomes meaningless. Myth makes human suffering tolerable by giving it transhistorical significance.

Faulkner's effort to remythologize the South in his Yoknapatawpha fiction is an attempt, through the medium of literary art, to construct a new bridge to the larger spiritual reality which shapes human destiny. Though he always feared that the consciously wrought myth of art was a mere illusory escape from the bleak reality of history, he continued to search for a unifying religious vision which would give history meaning. This religious quest first takes shape in *The Sound and the Fury*, where Faulkner concludes the three failed attempts of the Compson brothers to tell Caddy's story with a fourth mythic narrative. As we shall see, this fourth effort also falls short of religious affirmation, but the quest begun there continues in all of Faulkner's great fiction and meets finally with qualified success in *Go Down, Moses*.

The key for an understanding of *The Sound and the Fury* and *Absalom, Absalom!* is to be found in an introduction to *The Sound and the Fury* which Faulkner wrote but never published.[9] The Southern writer, he says, has two equally violent tendencies, to indict his society and to escape it. In *The Sound and the Fury*, he adds, he did both at one time. What I think Faulkner means by this cryptic remark is that his novel exposes a corrupt Southern aristocracy in its death agony, and that, in fashioning from this material a work of art, he was escaping the very milieu in which he lived. If we view the novel in these terms (and in this instance I think Faulkner can be trusted as a reliable commentator on his own work), it becomes impossible to separate whatever lessons he has to teach us from what he has to say about the South. Further, these twin aims of indictment and escape leave no room for reclamation or repair of the Southern tradition. Faulkner cannot be, from this perspective, an enlightened Southerner who criticizes the excesses of his society by calling for a return to its best traditions; he must instead remain an artist who exposes the cancer at the very core of his culture, and who seeks to detach himself from the diseased organism.

The fact that Faulkner here speaks of his attempt to indict and escape the South as an artistic venture is crucial for understanding his work. On the one

---

[8]*The Myth of the Eternal Return or Cosmos and History* (Princeton: Princeton University Press, 1954; paper repr. 1974).
[9]*A Faulkner Miscellany*, James B. Meriwether, ed. (Jackson: University of Mississippi Press, 1974), 156–61.

hand, it is clear that Faulkner viewed art as a spiritual enterprise with social consequences. In his judgment "the writer unconsciously writes into every line and phrase his violent despairs and rages and frustrations or his violent prophecies of still more violent hopes."[10] The artist thus struggles at the personal level with questions of meaning which have larger cultural significance.

Faulkner implies that the answers his culture has given to such questions are faulty, and that it therefore becomes the lot of the writer to take on the role of prophet. One is reminded here of Shelley's claim that poets are the unacknowledged legislators of the world; Faulkner's conception of the artist indeed owes much to the Romantic tradition.[11] But Faulkner also maintains that art is an escape from the spiritual malaise and moral ambiguity of social life in the South. In describing his state of mind when he wrote his first great novel, Faulkner makes clear that the composition of *The Sound and the Fury* was an act of utter love which was complete and satisfying in itself. The image of "the muddy bottom of a little doomed girl climbing a blooming pear tree in April" was for him nothing less than a religious icon. It provided him access to a universe of beauty and truth which was not available in the sordid actuality of everyday life. While the material for his "Tyrrhenian vase" is taken from the mud of a corrupt society, his art transforms it into an image of purity and beauty.

In our examination of *The Sound and the Fury* and *Absalom, Absalom!* we shall see two of the ways in which Faulkner carried out this project. But, having made this case for the religious function of his art, we must add the immediate qualification that he was never certain that art could adequately fill the spiritual void which he discerned. In his introduction to *The Sound and the Fury* he confesses that the escape made possible by art may be merely "sentimental." He fears that art may be a means of avoiding a despair so deep that it cannot be directly overcome. Faulkner was throughout his career troubled by the suspicion that literature did not provide an authentic alternative to the absence of meaning in modern culture, that it allowed one merely to indulge the comforting illusion of having found such an alternative. In reading his work, we must bear in mind not only the degree to which it is informed by a desire to forge religious meaning but also his deep-seated doubt that art could perform this feat.

---

[10] Meriwether, 158.
[11] Faulkner's Romantic conception of the artist has been extensively documented in recent scholarly work on his early poetry. See, for example, Lewis P. Simpson, "Sex and History: Origins of Faulkner's Apocrypha" in *The Maker and the Myth: Faulkner and Yoknapatawpha* (Jackson: University of Mississippi Press, 1978), 122–45 and Minter, 75ff.

II

Quentin Compson is perhaps the most important character in Faulkner's fiction. Not only does he figure prominently in Faulkner's two best known novels, but he is in himself the most complex and curious of Faulkner's narrators. His proximity in age, social position, and verbal brilliance to his creator indicates that Faulkner invested a great deal of himself in this character. Given this fact, it is surprising that Quentin is not the protagonist of either of the novels in which he appears. Both *The Sound and the Fury* and *Absalom, Absalom!* instead have at their centers a silent figure who is not allowed to tell his or her own story. In fact, the driving motive behind the narrative of each novel is an effort to tell the story of this figure. Critics have always appreciated the degree to which this is true of *Absalom, Absalom!*, and recent interpretations have made the same point concerning *The Sound and the Fury*.[12] The narrators of *The Sound and the Fury* are attempting with only partial success to tell how and why Caddy failed to accomplish what was expected of her, just as *Absalom, Absalom!* consists of unsuccessful efforts to describe and explain Sutpen's tragedy. Though Caddy's centrality is partially obscured by the difficulties of Jason and Quentin, surely Faulkner is correct when he says of the earlier novel that in it he tried four times to tell a single story, and that it was the story of the "doomed girl."

We have, then, at least two reasons for considering these novels as companion pieces in a larger artistic endeavor. In both Quentin Compson is a prominent character and narrator, and in each novel he and his fellow narrators are attempting to tell the story of a compelling but silent central figure. But there is a third and decisive reason for regarding these novels as complementary: each discloses the failure of the Southern myth to provide an acceptable model for human interaction. The social roles which the myth does provide are morally flawed, and they create an ethical and religious tension which is finally irresolvable.

A major element of Caddy's tragedy is the repressive role which she as a well-born white woman is assigned in Southern society. Likewise, Sutpen's downfall is the inevitable outcome of his attempt to live according to the flawed model of the Southern male aristocrat. And in each case the tragedy that results from a distorting cultural paradigm embraces not merely one life, or even the effect of one life on a single community, but an entire tradition.

---

[12] For a thorough but thin treatment of this topic see Catherine B. Baum, "The Beautiful One: Caddy Compson as Heroine of *the Sound and the Fury*" in *William Faulkner: The Compson Family*, Arthur F. Kinney, ed. (Boston: G.K. Hall & Co., 1982), 186–96. For a more succinct and penetrating statement see David Minter, *William Faulkner: His Life and Work* (Baltimore: Johns Hopkins University Press, 1980) 96–97.

The fragmented narratives which Faulkner weaves around Caddy and Sutpen locate the deeper tragedy of Yoknapatawpha in the collapse of those structures of meaning which make human action comprehensible. This deeper tragedy is best recorded in the sections of the novels narrated by Quentin Compson, for he is the character most sensitive to it. In the larger scheme of Faulkner's work, these novels point beyond the destruction of their protagonists to the greater cultural breakdown which the smaller tragedies reflect. Quentin is the character who struggles with this deeper crisis, and his inability to tell the stories of Caddy and Sutpen as a convincing whole points to the real tragedy of *The Sound and the Fury* and *Absalom, Absalom!*.

Quentin has aptly been called Faulkner's Hamlet.[13] Like Shakespeare's character, Quentin finds himself in what Alasdair MacIntyre has styled an "epistemological crisis."[14] The problem which confronts him is how to discover, amidst all the explanations pressing in upon him, the one that accurately describes the reality which he faces. Narrative becomes problematic for him because the interpretative framework which he has inherited has been called into question. As is the case with Hamlet, the crisis he cannot avoid is at bottom religious. If the human world is indeed fabricated from a tissue of lies, where does one place that basic trust which allows one to reclaim meaning? The epistemological dilemma into which Quentin is thrust destroys that essential faith in a dependable reality without which human life lapses into chaos. Quentin Compson is obsessed with "telling the story," first of his sister Caddy, then of Thomas Sutpen. This task is urgent for him because, as we shall see, his own identity is at stake. His failure to tell the story successfully reflects the inadequacy of the explanatory models his society has provided him. This failure provokes a spiritual crisis which Quentin is unable to resolve except by taking his own life.

In *The Sound and the Fury* and *Absalom, Absalom!* Faulkner has given testimony to the heavy burden which the breakdown of traditional structures of history, value, and meaning places on the human spirit. As we chart the course of Quentin Compson's journey in search of meaning, we shall discover the depth of Faulkner's indictment of the culture which shaped him, and the means by which he hoped to escape it.

---

[13]*Vide* Michel Gresset, "The Ordeal of Consciousness" in Kinney, 175, and William R. Taylor, *Cavalier and Yankee* (New York: Doubleday Anchor Books, 1963), 137-40.

[14]For a penetrating insight into Hamlet that applies equally well to Quentin, see Alasdair MacIntyre, "Epistemological Crises, Dramatic Narrative, and the Philosophy of Science" in *Paradigms and Revolutions,* Gary Gutting, ed. (Notre Dame: University of Notre Dame Press, 1980), 54–74.

III

Faulkner's ironic attack on the Southern romance of innocence begins in earnest with *The Sound and the Fury*. The first three sections of the novel are narrated by three brothers who, in relating the disintegration of their own lives, describe from their particular angle of vision the disintegration of the entire Compson clan. The point at which their private preoccupations merge is their sense of the central role that their sister Candace plays in the family history. Benjy's primitive consciousness is regularly jarred by reminders of the sister he loved above all else. The cry of "Caddy" on the neighboring golf course sends him into paroxysms of pain, for it reminds him that the one he associated with that name has left him. On the other hand, he draws consolation from the slipper she gave him because it revives the memory of those days when she was his constant companion. In his mind even olfactory sensations carry associations with Caddy. The nurturing sister "smelled like trees"; the perfume which she puts on for her first lover is for Benjy the sign of her betrayal of him (58).[15] Benjy is finally removed from the Compson household when he chases the school girls who remind him of Caddy but who mistake his eager approach for sexual aggressiveness.

Quentin is similarly obsessed with his sister; he broods constantly on her sexual impurity and his desire to absorb her dishonor into himself. Like Benjy he is at last accused of sexually molesting a little girl whom he calls "Sister" (161). This event is the immediate prelude to his suicide, which appears in part to be motivated by his inability to redeem his sister's honor.

Jason Compson lacks the love for his sister which his brothers share, but, like them, he attributes the poverty of his existence to her failings, telling himself that her promiscuity cost him the respectable job he would otherwise have had and that the illegitimate daughter she left behind is destroying what little good repute the family has retained. Jason's section of the novel ends when Caddy's daughter robs him of the hoard he has stolen from the women in his family as compensation for the damage he feels they have done him.

The narratives of Caddy's brothers which make up the first three sections of *The Sound and the Fury* have in common an apparent randomness which borders on incoherence. Each version of the Compsons' woes has a compulsive quality which distorts the flow of the narrative. Benjy, for example, is an idiot whose consciousness works exclusively by association of sense experience. He grieves over his absent sister without fully realizing that she is permanently lost to him. To Benjy, Caddy represents the nurturing, maternal woman whom he never found in his own mother. But he is unable to articu-

---

[15]*The Sound and the Fury* (New York: Random House, 1929; Vintage Books edition, 1954). All page references in the text are made to this edition.

late either his need for her or his loss of her. Benjy's is indeed a tale told by an idiot, poignant but vacuous.

Quentin's section stands at the extreme opposite from Benjy's. So completely self-conscious is Quentin that his every attempt to enter the stream of life comes to nought. Benjy is incapable of abstraction; Quentin is capable of hardly anything else. History, the actual realm of the changing world, is his enemy. In his obsession with Caddy, Quentin seeks to cancel time, to erase the connection with the ongoing process of life and death which her sexuality symbolizes. But Quentin can only succeed in this effort by severing the bond between consciousness and reality altogether. The disjointed discourse which characterizes his section of the novel remains a series of repetitions with no real movement or point; his narrative fails to bring the events of the novel into a coherent pattern. By denying time and Caddy's sexuality Quentin repudiates life. His attempt to commit incest with his sister is prompted by his desire to absorb her sexuality into himself, and so annul history. When this effort fails, he removes himself from time by the only other means available to him, which is suicide.

Jason, as Faulkner says in the appendix, is the "sanest" of the Compsons, and thus his narrative has a certain kind of continuity. But Jason's view of life is so narrow and ungenerous that he is incapable of discerning the true causes of the Compsons' misery. He supposes that the Compsons have been undone by their failure to reckon with the primacy of self-interest in human affairs. The family honor which is of great importance to Quentin is for Jason of no consequence at all. Caddy's promiscuity is, from Jason's point of view, simply the result of her uncontrollable animal lust. He hates her because she has thwarted the scheme by which he could satisfy his own lust for money; and in his eyes, avarice is the only rational principle of conduct. He considers Benjy to be merely a defective sibling who ought to be removed from the Compson household, and Quentin he regards as a spoiled idealist who did the world a favor by bringing his life to an end.

Despite the objective scheme into which Jason is able to place the events of the novel, his narrative is as compulsive and unsatisfactory as his brothers'. Uncle Job says that Jason is too smart to keep up with himself, and Jason's narrative bears him out. While Jason has a ready and coherent interpretation of Caddy's actions, it is an interpretation that does not really explain anything. So absorbed is he in his own acquisitiveness that he is unable to understand the very different motives which drive his siblings. This "realist" who is confident that he understands his niece is in fact outwitted by her when she robs him in his absence. He sees acquisitiveness as the basic human characteristic, but he cannot in these terms account for the terrible defeat which has overtaken his entire family.

Faulkner declares in the appendix that Jason finally succeeded in ridding himself of the Compson curse, but at the price of cutting himself off entirely from his family and its history. So alien is his mercantile mindset to the Southern aristocratic tradition, and so obtuse is he with respect to the spiritual problems which plague the Compsons that he is incapable of taking anything like a full measure of Caddy's tragedy. Indeed, none of the brothers is able to bring order to time or to find any principle of coherence in the fall of the Compson house.

IV

The narratives which compose *The Sound and the Fury* are incoherent because the woman who figures so prominently in them does not fit the social-psychological role she is assigned.[16] Though each of her brothers views her differently, none is able to comprehend the concrete actuality that she represents, and thus all their stories are tales of sound and fury, signifying nothing.

The role which Caddy is expected to play but cannot perform is that of the idealized Southern white woman. The white woman, as countless newspaper editorials and political speeches in the South from antebellum times well into this century have asserted, is the vessel of Southern virtue. Her function is to epitomize the gentility, decorum, and moral rectitude which represent the height of civilization. But, as Richard King has made clear in his discussion of the Southern family romance as manifest particularly in the work of Lillian Smith, the positive side of this model is cancelled by the negative.[17] In the romance of innocence which serves as the South's foundational myth, the role of the white woman masks the aggressive drive for mastery that is the real motive behind the basic social structures of traditional Southern culture.

The realm of moral purity presided over by the white woman is made culturally necessary by the expectation that the white male will sully his hands in the affairs of the world. In his role as provider he is expected to make those compromises with his conscience which are necessary to achieve economic success. Moreover, the hidden and unacknowledged code says that his libido will seek satisfaction outside the marital bond. The official code, on the other hand, dictates that the white woman maintain her sexual purity as an emblem of the prevailing moral norm.

---

[16] Daniel Joseph Singal, *The War Within: From Victorian to Modernist Thought in the South, 1919–1945* (Chapel Hill: University of North Carolina Press, 1982), 176.

[17] Although it is directed at the work of Lillian Smith, Richard King's treatment of the role of women in the Southern family romance on 185–93, *A Southern Renaissance* brilliantly illuminates Caddy's role in *The Sound and the Fury*.

The white woman's role is further defined by the complementary role of the black woman. The black woman is supposed to be a sexually promiscuous creature, and thus the permissible object of the white man's passion. The black woman also supervises the nurture of white children, since their aloof natural mothers abdicate this responsibility. The black woman in the Southern family romance thus represents the passionate sexuality and maternal care which the white woman cannot display in the ethereal realm to which she is consigned. The white woman is supposed to be a creature of refined feminine sentiment, but not of passion. She is removed both from the sphere of animal instinct and that of physical labor.

In *The Sound and the Fury* these basic feminine roles are all represented. Mrs. Compson is the archetypal white Southern woman gone to seed. She has removed herself both from the sexual embrace of her husband and from a nurturing relationship to her children. She is a hypochondriac who fears the violation of her body by disease. She naively entrusts her financial affairs to her shiftless brother and her unscrupulous son. Her primary concern is for the family honor of which she considers herself to be the custodian, but her efforts to preserve it are quaint and ineffective. She has removed herself so completely from the world of passion and action that she has withered into a neurasthenia that renders her utterly incompetent in every sphere of life.

The black houseservant Dilsey, on the other hand, is the adhesive that holds the Compson family together. She provides such nurture as the children receive, and she is the most perceptive and the wisest character in the novel. While Dilsey's sexuality is not treated in the novel, her hearty engagement in the other processes of life and death suggests that she is no stranger to sexual passion.

Caddy must be understood against the backdrop of the feminine roles exemplified by her mother and Dilsey. She is able to fill neither, and so becomes first an irritant in the cultural structure, and then an outcast. Her tragedy is the result of a role reversal in which she tries to bring into the white woman's world the sexual passion and maternal nurture assigned to the black woman. To succeed in this venture would be to overturn the social order, but to fail at it would be to lapse into her mother's pathetic condition.

The younger Compsons suffer from having a mother who is unable to care for her children or to provide them with emotional stability. Mrs. Compson feels it to be an insult that her first-born is mentally retarded, and she alters his name when it is clear that he he will never be normal. She repeatedly shifts responsibility for the children between Dilsey and her husband, then claims that both undermine her maternal authority. None of her children is able to confide in her; her reaction to every difficulty is to retire to her sickroom.

As a result of their mother's neuroticism, the children are left in an emotional vacuum. Dilsey does what she can to fill it, but she lacks the social status that would allow her to be a mother to the Compson children in the full sense. Caddy therefore becomes "mother" to her brothers by default. When Benjy is rejected by his mother, it is Caddy to whom he turns. Quentin similarly comes to depend on Caddy as his confidant and counselor. Jason, who is Caddy's enemy, hates her precisely because she assumes the authority of the mother in their family circle. Even in childhood games, Caddy is the one who wants to be in charge and who is most capable of exercising authority.

In becoming "mother" to her brothers, Caddy is assuming the role abdicated by her mother, as she is also incorporating the black mammy's function into the duties of the white woman. Her mother, always the guardian of genteel manners, chides Caddy for "pampering" Benjy. Her intimacy with Benjy and Quentin is unseemly from Mrs. Compson's perspective. It is the job of Negroes to attend to the physical needs of children. But there is another and stronger force which prevents Caddy's becoming "mother" to her brothers: her own sexuality.

Though their motives are very different, both Benjy and Quentin resent Caddy's sexual liberation. Benjy takes the new scent Caddy wears to mean that she is no longer part of the natural world to which he belongs (where "Caddy smelled like trees"), and he utters an ear-bursting howl of protest. Quentin views Caddy's first love affair as a violation of their relationship and an affront to the family honor, and he attempts to avenge her betrayal in a number of desperate acts, none of them successful.

The point of immediate import is that by giving herself to a passionate sexuality Caddy is violating the mores governing Southern white women, just as she also defies the cultural code in becoming a mother to her brothers. The cultural ideal denied sexual passion to the white woman altogether. The institution of marriage was supposed to insure pure bloodlines and control the inheritance of property. Caddy fails on both counts. By having an affair she gives in to animal passion, and, by telling her husband that the child she is carrying may not be his, she disrupts the social and economic arrangement which binds her family to his.

The novel wants to suggest, however, that Caddy's presumed shortcomings really point to the unsatisfactoriness of the cultural standards by which she is judged. Like the heroine of Kate Chopin's *The Awakening,* Caddy's "sins" are acts of protest against a social code which stifles the human spirit. For her the life of a kept woman offers the only avenue of escape from an insular society; conformity to the model represented by her mother seems to promise nothing but the denial of her humanity.

The social indictment implicit in Faulkner's treatment of Caddy's promiscuity may also be discerned in his treatment of her relationship to her brothers. Caddy's brothers turn to her for emotional support because their weak and defeated parents are unable to provide any kind of stability for their children. The Compsons are quite literally living on the dwindling capital of their past. They are unable to reconcile the aristocratic code of honor with the new mercantile culture which is the order of the day. As a result, the Compsons are insular and insecure. The children (Jason the exception as always) are thrown upon themselves. Their reaction to this situation is to build a psychological barrier which will exclude all others from their self-sufficient circle.

Benjy and Quentin fear Caddy's sexuality because it threatens to thrust her outside the family sphere and thus to destroy the sustaining if artificial cocoon they have built around themselves. Quentin attempts (as does Benjy to a limited degree) to head off the threat to his claim on Caddy by offering himself as her sexual partner. It is crucial to see that Quentin feels no sexual desire for his sister; instead, he longs forever to seal off himself and his sister from the intrusions of an alien world. Quentin's one attempt to commit incest is quite pathetic. He tries clumsily to seduce his sister, and fails. He then endeavors to kill her with a phallic thrust of his knife, and though Caddy commands him to complete the act, he cannot. Later, when Quentin confesses to his father the crime he did not commit, he describes the chamber in hell to which he hopes he and his sister will be committed (97f). The unthinkable thought for Quentin is not that they will suffer such a fate, but that they will escape it because of the cowardice which prevented him from accomplishing his incestuous design.

Quentin's "incestuous" desires are thus motivated by his need to protect the psychological womb which the Compsons inhabit. He wants to sleep with his sister in order to prevent her seeking a sexual partner outside the family circle. And, paradoxically, Quentin thinks that an incestuous relation with Caddy will preserve the family honor. By violating the universal taboo and suffering the expected eternal punishment for that deed, Quentin hopes negatively to demonstrate that *something* is sacred, and that the Compsons are respectful of it. Quentin is thus driven to the extremity of attempting incest in order to preserve the cultural structure into which he was born.

V

As defender of the family honor, Quentin plays a crucial part in Faulkner's indictment of Southern culture. Of all the Compson children he alone seeks to preserve the aristocratic tradition into which they were born. He is sent to Harvard precisely because he is expected to become the bearer of the family standard when his father dies. In the novel he represents the self-conscious Southern aristocrat who is attempting to sustain his way of life.[18] By

---

[18] See Singal, 176; see also John Hunt, "The Disappearance of Quentin Compson" in Kinney, 375.

demonstrating Quentin's inability to sustain even his own life, Faulkner exposes the spiritual poverty of the entire Southern tradition. His attempt at incest is born of a desire to preserve the tradition of which he is the guardian. Caddy's sexuality is the great threat to the mythic structure which undergirds Quentin's entire world-view.

We have seen how the Southern white woman was denied sexual passion in order to maintain the ideals of purity and innocence. Since Quentin cannot extinguish Caddy's sexuality, he attempts to bend it in upon himself, and thus contain it. If he can achieve this, he will have at least denied the power of passion to break family bonds. Further, he will have proved that he controls the family's honor. By causing Caddy's disgrace himself, he will have asserted his ability to destroy the honor he cannot protect. Quentin's incestuous fixation reflects a perverse desire to establish the reality of honor by violating it.

That Quentin's attempt at incest is but one of many efforts to defend Caddy's honor should be readily apparent. His showdown with Dalton Ames is clearly meant to accomplish the same purpose as his incestuous encounter with his sister. He objects to the man Caddy marries on the grounds that he is not honorable, for Herbert, Caddy's intended, has been kicked out of Harvard for cheating. Quentin's futile attack on Gerald Bland is another example of psychological displacement: its true motive is the desire to champion his sister's honor. But as his conversations with his father demonstrate, the very concept of honor has in the South of the twentieth century become problematic.

In his fatherly admonitions to his son, Mr. Compson tells Quentin that honor is a word that has meaning only in the games men play amongst themselves. He argues that female virginity, the symbol of honor so precious to men, is but a "fragile membrane" which means nothing to women and should not be taken too seriously by Quentin. And though he intends to pierce the illusions of Quentin's youthful inexperience, what he says has instead the effect of deepening his son's despair. For if Mr. Compson is correct, then not only is Caddy's behavior a matter of indifference, but the whole set of values by which he has taught Quentin to live is a sham. Mr. Compson is correct when he tells Quentin, "It's nature is hurting you not Caddy," but the inability to reconcile nature and value is precisely Quentin's difficulty (144). Quentin draws the conclusion which his father resists: namely, that if honor has no reality outside the arbitrary social etiquette prescribed by the Southern myth, it is ultimately without any meaning at all. But since Quentin is unwilling to accept such a conclusion, he persists in his struggle to breathe some bit of life into the dying code.

The attempt to live within the framework of the myth which sponsors the code of honor leads Quentin into a state of delusion. When he plays the part of chivalrous champion he is met not only with defeat but with scorn. Dalton

Ames tells Quentin that women are all alike and not worth defending. Gerald Blanton, while playing the part of Southern gallant, parodies the role by making fools of the women who flock to him. In perhaps the most telling irony of all, Quentin is accused of molesting an immigrant girl whom he has defended by her irrate older brother. In every situation in which Quentin finds himself the gap is revealed between his code of honor and the social reality it is meant to explain.

Only in the psychological world completely under his control can Quentin hope to make the code work. Since he cannot live by this high standard in a society that no longer recognizes it, he attempts to confine his social world to the family. Incest is an effort to make Caddy an extension of himself. It is a strategy which fails because Caddy refuses to become absorbed into Quentin's consciousness. She is willing to die for Quentin but not to deny her sexuality in order to endorse the code of honor in which Quentin wants to believe.

Caddy remains outside the only categories by which Quentin could make her story meaningful. She stands as living proof of Mr. Compson's assertion that women are not the Madonnas men have made of them, but are instead cunning animals. As a result, Quentin is finally forced to admit that honor itself is illusory, and that the Southern myth is discredited; he refuses to live in a world where they are meaningless. He is incapable of easing into the alcoholic cynicism of his father, and the only other option open to him is suicide.

VI

The centrality of Dilsey in the last section of *The Sound and the Fury* is manifest, and many have argued that through the Christian view of time which she holds and the redemptive experience she enjoys on Easter morning, Faulkner finds order and meaning in the chaotic events which have destroyed the Compson family. Faulkner, on this view, shares Dilsey's Christian presuppositions, albeit from a more sophisticated vantage point.[19] But Faulkner's attitude toward Dilsey's Christianity is more ambiguous than this interpretation suggests. It is true that Faulkner holds Dilsey up as a model of sanity and spiritual strength, and that she is in every way the most admirable character in the novel. There is good reason to believe, however, that Faulkner finds Dilsey's perspective on the Compsons as unsatisfactory as those represented by Caddy's brothers. Using a rhetorical strategy which he will

---

[19]Amos Wilder, "Vestigial Moralities in *The Sound and the Fury*" in *Religious Perspectives in Faulkner's Fiction*, J. Robert Barth, ed. (Notre Dame: University of Notre Dame Press, 1972), 102.

repeat throughout his career, Faulkner in this section creates the illusion of religious meaning only to withdraw his allegiance to it.

Faulkner begins his final attempt to tell Caddy's story by casting Dilsey in a mythic light. She emerges from her cabin on Easter morning as a noble and solitary figure who proceeds to establish human order in the new day that has come to the old earth. Her movements are at once in harmony with the rhythms of the morning and bent toward pulling the recalcitrant Compson household into timely order. Her time is *kairos*: meaningful, divinely ordered time. She works industriously but not frantically. Having done all that she can to restore order after Jason's discovery of Miss Quentin's thievery, Dilsey leads her own children and Ben in a stately procession to the Negro church. There she is transported into a state of rapture by the Rev. Shegog's evocation of "the recollection and the blood of the Lamb" (367). At the end of the sermon she declares that she has seen the first and the last, by which she means that she has had a glimpse of the Alpha and Omega in the light of which one may believe in the ultimate redemption of human suffering.

Dilsey's religious epiphany appears to bring the tragedy of the Compsons to a not wholly negative resolution. The hatred and death that have swallowed up the Compson household are conquered by the promise of the Resurrection. The fragmented tales of the previous narrators are subsumed in the "recollection" which sees the first and the last, the new life bursting forth in the trees that surround the Compson dwellings testifying to life's eternal promise. It would seem that here the Christian myth has redeemed history.

Faulkner's handling of these events, however, undercuts Dilsey's affirmation. The entire church scene is painted as an aesthetic production which serves the imagination but does not answer the bleak negativity of history. The church itself is described as a "painted cardboard set on the ultimate edge of the flat earth . . . " (364). Throughout the section an uncommon amount of attention is given to dress. Dilsey herself appears first in her Easter regalia, then in her work clothes, then in her Sunday finery again. Luster insists on wearing his new hat and Frony her best dress despite the threat of rain.

The master of appearances, however, is the Rev. Shegog. Unlike the congregation's regular preacher his countenance is unimposing; he looks, indeed, like a monkey. The medium of Shegog's art is the spoken word. His preaching is described as a performance in which he is like "a man on a tight rope" (366). Even his rhetoric takes on the character of a balancing act as he alternates between two seemingly incongruous dialects. When he begins his sermon, he sounds like a white man, but at the climax of his sermon he switches into the Negro idiom and begins an incantation, the refrain of which is "de ricklickshun en de Blood of de Lamb".

The effect of the service on Dilsey is thus the result of an artistic production. The magician-like Shegog has changed the mundane into the mysterious; art has transformed the meaningless into the significant. We are left wondering, however, whether we have been edified or entertained. As Lewis Simpson has pointed out, the self-conscious act of the Rev. Shegog "suggests an ambivalent relation between revealed truth and history, between the eternal and the temporal."[20] Dilsey's declaration thus has the ironic effect of throwing the reader back into the unredeemed drama of the Compsons, "the last" of whom has just departed the family circle with a circus hustler.

Faulkner's treatment of this scene is not intended to cast doubts on the authenticity of black peasant Christianity, but rather to question the validity of any religious vision that might redeem the Compson tragedy. Dilsey is an admirable character whose faith is genuine and whose wisdom is great. If even her affirmation is based on the illusion created by a cleverly staged theatrical production, the joke is finally on anyone who would preserve the virtues she embodies. While Faulkner treats Dilsey herself with deep sympathy and respect, the theatrical metaphors he employs in describing the occasion of her religious epiphany reveal his deep ambivalence towards the Christian vision which sponsors her faith. Faulkner seems to envy Dilsey her faith, but to be unable to emulate it.

The note on which the novel ends is not the apocalyptic evocation of the Resurrection which the Rev. Shegog achieves, but the absurd bellowing of the idiot Benjy, who is outraged that his customary clockwise revolution around the Court House Square has been reversed. Faulkner in effect cancels out Dilsey's redemptive reliance on the Resurrection by returning us to a social reality in which order and meaning are defined by the arbitrary designation of right rather than left as the proper direction in which to circle a pigeon-stained Civil War monument. The point of this juxtaposition, like the impact of Dalton Ames' casual quashing of Quentin's attempt to play the role of Caddy's chivalric avenger, is to expose the gap between any system of values and the brutish reality it is meant to explain. However hopeful the promise claimed by Dilsey that our tears will be wiped away and all things made new, Faulkner jerks us back to an absurd reality that is thoroughly immune to redemption.

The place of Dilsey's Christianity in the novel is comparable to her status as measured against the other powerful female figure in the Compson household, Caddy. Unlike the other sections of *The Sound and the Fury,* the final one mentions Caddy hardly at all. Instead, it dwells on the aftermath of her tragedy, and is a kind of denouement which leaves us with an image of the empty shell the Compson household has become since her departure. Just as in her childhood Caddy assumed the role of mother to her brothers, and thus displaced Mrs. Compson as keeper of the hearth, so Dilsey, once Caddy

---

[20]Simpson, *The Brazen Face of History,* 207.

leaves, assumes the role that both white women have abdicated. But in a racist society it is impossible for Dilsey to become matron of a white family in any complete sense. Southern mores prohibit her from occupying a social position reserved for white women, and so Dilsey cannot fully replace either Mrs. Compson or Caddy. Instead, her maternal wisdom and perseverance serve to indict her white counterparts by contrast.

Dilsey's virtues are important because they expose the failings of the Compson women. She represents that wholesome integration of genuine maternal concern and healthy earthiness which is lacking in the role assigned white women. She achieves in her own social niche what it is impossible for Caddy to accomplish in hers. The point of the contrast is once again to illustrate the degree to which Caddy's tragedy is a cultural failure. Dilsey is an admirable figure precisely because she has made use of those feminine qualities which Southern culture has allowed her as a black woman and denied Caddy as a white woman. Dilsey's success thus serves to indict Southern white culture for denying to Caddy the ingredients of that success.

Dilsey's Christianity, like her feminine virtues, is presented in the novel as a noble achievement, but one unavailable to the more sophisticated white world. The Rev. Shegog's sermon is emotional, intuitive, and impressionistic. Dilsey responds with a faith which Faulkner does not conceive to be possible for those in the state of alienated self-consciousness which characterizes the Compsons. Although the preacher's religious language is full of evocative power, it has none of the rational force required to answer the questions of a Quentin. Faulkner, while he is drawn to the poetry of Negro religiosity, cannot accept its substance as convincing.[21] In the terrible either/or which will continue to haunt Faulkner's fiction, self-conscious rationality and poetic feeling stand antithetically opposed. Like Dilsey herself, Christianity in the novel serves as a healthy counter to the spiritual ills of Southern culture, but Faulkner can embrace it only as an aesthetic possibility.

No other character in the Compson household has Dilsey's religious faith and none possesses the fruits that derive from it. Her Christian perspective comes closest to integrating the total story into an intelligible whole, for hers is a world-view more coherent than that of any other character in the novel. Yet her religious vision is part of an older, mythic world-view which the progress of history has destroyed.[22] Dilsey's presence in the story serves to

---

[21] *Vide* Eric J. Sundquist, *Faulkner: The House Divided* (Baltimore: Johns Hopkins Univeristy Press, 1983), 13. Sundquist claims that "readers have only accepted the revival sermon of the 'monkey' preacher in Dilsey's section because they are taken in by its pose of cathartic naturalism." Although in my view Sundquist is insensitive to Faulkner's deep regard for Negro religiosity, I share his conclusion that for Faulkner Dilsey's Christianity is essentially a pose.

[22] Minter, "Notes on Faulkner and Creativity" in *Faulkner and the Southern Renaissance*, Fowler and Abadie, eds. (Jackson: University of Mississippi Press, 1981), 262.

illumine by contrast the depths to which the Compsons and their tradition have sunk. The intent of this contrast is not to call the South or the reader to a primitive though noble faith such as Dilsey's, but to expose the spiritual vacuity which apostasy prepares.

Indeed, the rhetorical strategy which Faulkner employs in the final section of *The Sound and the Fury* recurs throughout his work. He "escapes" (as he observed in the unpublished introduction with which we began) to a fictive world of mythic time whose patterns of meaning are utterly different from those of the "real" world. Through his art Faulkner imaginatively enters a perspective which Dilsey literally adopts. The crucial difference between author and character here is that, for Faulkner, Dilsey's Christianity is a pleasing fiction, whereas for Dilsey it is an accurate account of reality. Faulkner gropes to find a redemptive element in the Compsons' demise but rejects as unconvincing the single testimony of religious affirmation which the novel offers. Though art is capable of creating the illusion of meaning (just as, in different ways the code of honor and Christianity are able to do), its spell must be finally broken. Faulkner's tale, as he asserted, remains incomplete and fragmented. He fails to give his novel coherence not through lack of skill, but because, like his narrators, he lacks the framework that would allow him to explain and to transcend the chaotic cultural situation he confronted. The story remains a tale of "sound and fury, signifying nothing."

Viewed in this way, *The Sound and the Fury* becomes the four-part anatomy of a society in the midst of a calamitous spiritual crisis. The novel begins and ends with the indictment of a corrupt cultural order from the innocent perspective of first an idiot, and then a primitive Christian, neither of whom recognizes the radical separation between human values and the brute reality of social and physical life. The more sophisticated narrators take this gap as an inexorable and horrible fact of human existence and seek either to deny it (as does Quentin) or to embrace it (as does Jason). The occasion for this crisis of religious meaning is the breakdown of the white feminine model expressed in the life of Caddy, who is the novel's silent center. While Faulkner's sympathies certainly lie with Benjy and Dilsey, his own perception of the truth is closer to the views of Quentin and Jason. In *The Sound and the Fury* he is unable to find a home for human value to replace the shattered ideal of the pure and virginal woman. He leaves us with Benjy's bitter, inarticulate denunciation of a culture which rests on an illusion and with a universe which is totally hostile to the human project. Faulkner's quest for a new myth which will restore religious meaning to history remains incomplete.

CHAPTER 2

REJECTION OF THE MALE IDEAL AND THE BURDEN OF HISTORY: *ABSALOM, ABSALOM!*

In *The Sound and the Fury* Faulkner implicitly indicts Southern culture as a whole in exploring the failure of the Southern cultural model for white women—a failure strikingly exemplified by the case of Caddy Compson. In *Absalom, Absalom!* he works toward a similar end in examining the failure of the complementary male ideal. And the fact that in both works Quentin Compson is the most important of the several narrators who attempt to fathom the deeds of the silent figure dominating the action of the tale underscores the thematic parallel. But, of the two novels, *Absalom, Absalom!* is much the more capacious and the more frightening, precisely because as a mature, empire-building father, Sutpen has an historical importance which the doomed and adolescent Caddy does not have. Caddy *reflects* the culture which bred her, but Sutpen helped to create that culture: he is, in the full sense, a progenitor.

From its first conception Faulkner intended *Absalom, Absalom!* to serve as a companion piece to *The Sound and the Fury,* and very early in the process of composition he appears to have located the thematic heart of the tale in the juxtaposition of Sutpen's deeds and Quentin's words. Part of a diptych,

Absalom, Absalom! is a curiously "double" work itself, a work divided between words and deeds, but also between ideals and actions, between past and present, between fathers and sons, and between black and white. Even the title of the novel is double. And this doubleness suggests not only the divided mind of Quentin Compson as unwilling legatee of the past, and not only the ambivalence of Faulkner himself who both is and is not Quentin Compson (as Quentin is and is not Henry Sutpen): it also hints at Faulkner's own painfully mixed feelings about the South and its myth.

Faulkner's attitude is best revealed by a comment appearing in a letter written to his editor Hal Smith in June, 1933. He explains that he has placed Quentin "just before he is to commit suicide because of his sister," in order to "use the bitterness which he has projected on the South in the form of hatred of it and its people to get more out of the story itself" than might be expected of an "historical novel."[1] The connections between this statement of Faulkner's basic intentions in *Absalom, Absalom!* and the goals expressed in his unpublished preface to *The Sound and the Fury* are unmistakable. Though Faulkner here attributes to Quentin the bitterness which he himself feels toward the South, it is plain that he sees *Absalom, Absalom!* as an indictment of Southern culture which deepens and completes the indictment begun in *The Sound and the Fury*. This thematic connection is expressed not only through Quentin's serving as narrator in both novels but also in the fact that it is his despair over his sister which motivates Quentin's hatred of the South. Caddy exemplifies the world which Sutpen has symbolically made, and thus she stands as his spiritual heir.

If Quentin's situation in *Absalom, Absalom!* derives from the events of *The Sound and the Fury,* the tale which he tells in the later novel explains how the world of the earlier work came to be. The organic relation is plain: the fruit of the past is present misery, and present misery is the blighted result of poisoned roots lying far in the past. To maintain that Quentin's psychology and the "historical novel" embedded within *Absalom, Absalom!* are mutually enhancing is vastly to understate the case. Quentin's telling of Sutpen's tale binds past and present into an indissoluble unity which captures more than a century of Southern yearning and Southern woe, and thus his tale indicts a whole way of life. Quentin's psychological crisis not only reflects but ultimately derives from the crisis at the heart of Southern culture. His chagrin over the behavior of his sister and his uneasy probing of Sutpen's past reveal the dual failure of the traditional models as they apply both to men and to women, and suggest the utter bankruptcy of Southern ideals. In these novels Faulkner exposes the lie at the heart of the Southern cultural myth.

---

[1]*Selected Letters of William Faulkner,* Joseph Blotner, ed. (New York: Random House, 1977; Vintage Books Edition, 1978), 78–79.

Quentin, Faulkner's modern heir of the Southern aristocratic tradition, is in *Absalom, Absalom!* confronted with the fragments of a story which contains the secret of the founding of his culture. His obsession with this story, like his compulsive desire to contain his sister's sexuality, is rooted in his attempt at once to reappropriate the tradition which holds him and to break its grip upon him. Through his endeavor to reconstruct Thomas Sutpen's story, Quentin hopes to come to a full understanding of the tradition which he cannot ignore.

Indeed, with *Go Down, Moses,* this novel represents Faulkner's most profound exploration of historical myth. In Faulkner's view, history is not merely an impersonal sequence of events but the vital substance of the story wherein a people finds its identity and its basic values. For just this reason, historical myth is religious in its deepest intentionality; it serves indeed as a culture's charter of existence. So in *Absalom, Absalom!*, as in *Go Down, Moses,* Faulkner's meditation touches on the essentially religious foundations of Southern culture.

II

Shreve McCannon, the Canadian "outsider" who helps Quentin piece together Sutpen's story as the two of them huddle in a frigid Harvard dormitory room, is puzzled by a question that has troubled many readers of *Absalom, Absalom!*: namely, why is Quentin so obsessed with Sutpen? While Shreve himself finds Sutpen's saga interesting, for Quentin it has a personal importance which Shreve cannot fathom. Earlier, when Rosa Coldfield summons Quentin to her tomb-like dwelling and insists that he listen to her tale, she assigns to him a responsibility for discovering the truth about "the demon," a responsibility which he tacitly accepts. From Miss Rosa's perspective, Quentin is obliged to assist in this matter because Quentin's grandfather was Sutpen's friend, and Quentin has therefore inherited responsibility for Sutpen.

Miss Rosa's passionate hatred of "the demon" itself illumines Quentin's obsession. She despises him because in her view he was a traitor to the Southern cause which she continues to champion in heroic verse, and also because he insulted her by insisting that she produce a male heir as a precondition to marriage. She thinks of Sutpen as one who not only assaulted her dignity but who also imperilled her entire society. She is outraged by the thought that her fate should have depended on men like Sutpen: "men with valor and strength but without pity or honor." "Is it any wonder," she asks, "that Heaven saw fit to let us lose?" (57).[2]

---

[2]*Absalom, Absalom!* (New York: Random House, 1936; Modern Library Edition, 1964), 57. All future references are to this edition, and page numbers will be included in the text.

Miss Rosa speaks these words at the very beginning of *Absalom, Absalom!*, and, as the novel progresses, her assessment of Thomas Sutpen gains in plausibility. She believes that the failure of the South derived from the flawed character of men like Sutpen. He was a tower of strength and valor who clawed and stripped from the virgin earth a private kingdom of which he was total master, but he did so without pity or honor, and so offended the natural order which in the end rose up and destroyed him. Sutpen initially appears both to Quentin and Shreve—and to the reader—to be little more than a dark parody of the humane and refined Southern planter who is commonly presumed to have been the real founder and defender of the South. But, as the story continues and Mr. Compson, Quentin, and Shreve begin to succumb to its power, they come to share Rosa's sense of Sutpen's exemplary importance and of the demonic nature of his character. Quentin is obsessed with Sutpen's story because it contains the dark secret of the culture for which Quentin has inherited responsibility.

Critics often overlook the extent to which the power of *Absalom, Absalom!* depends on the reader's acknowledgment of Sutpen's story as emblematic of Southern history. Sutpen becomes a figure of heroic proportions worthy of comparison to the great Greek tragic heroes only insofar as we regard him as one whose fate summarizes that of his whole race. Indeed, Faulkner uses all of his powers as a storyteller to persuade the reader to see Sutpen as an heroic figure. And we are drawn into Sutpen's world by our increasing realization that to understand Sutpen is to understand the South.

Sutpen does not, of course, appear to fit the accepted model of the Southern planter. He rides into Jefferson in 1833 unknown and solitary, possessing little more than his clothes and his nearly empty saddlebags, and he proceeds to carve out a plantation for himself by dint of ruthlessness, good luck, and sheer unyielding will. He is able to gain a place in the community by marrying into a respectable family and by cultivating the friendship of Quentin's grandfather, but he remains an enigma to the town even after it finally grants him a wary respect. As his story unfolds we discover that he was born into an impoverished Appalachian family, has received almost no formal education, and is a thoroughly self-made man.

Sutpen therefore lacks nearly all of the identifying features of the Southern gentleman as represented by tradition. He can claim no genteel origins (in fact, he chooses to hide his past altogether); he has earned his wealth instead of inheriting it, and he can only ape the manners of the well-born. Cleanth Brooks describes Sutpen as a man who has won a place for himself through single-minded adherence to his "plan," but as one who remains a stranger within the community which has grudgingly accepted him. Sutpen's gentility, in short, is a thin and carefully constructed façade.[3]

Sutpen is significant, however, precisely because he exposes the falseness of the traditional ideal. His story calls into question both the historical accuracy of the accepted model and the values which lie behind it, and the novel does indeed want to assert that the human actuality of Southern life has been different from what popular conceptions would suggest. Sutpen is not an anomaly but an archetype, and a close examination of Sutpen's grand design and of the reasons for its failure discloses what is morally problematic in the entire array of values on which Southern culture has been based.

III

Quentin's description of Sutpen's childhood is the centerpiece of *Absalom, Absalom!*, and its dramatic power derives from the contrast between Sutpen as young innocent and the mature "demon" he finally becomes. The characteristics which mark the Sutpen of record are ruthlessness, strength, and indifference to public opinion: the episode in which he woos and marries Ellen Coldfield presents a typical case of the style of his behavior in Jefferson.

In an effort to consolidate his position in the town, Sutpen courts and wins the daughter of a respected local businessman. The people of Jefferson, however, are outraged at the prospect of the marriage: an outsider with no past that he will discuss is about to gain the legitimacy which only such a connection can confer. Though every respectable family in Jefferson is invited to the wedding, only Quentin's grandparents and the Coldfields attend. Meanwhile, the town rabble arms itself and assembles outside the church to wait for the ruckus into which they are certain the scandalous event will finally explode. But apart from a few rotten vegetables, no missiles are actually thrown because Sutpen prevents the crowd from acting. "[S]tanding there motionless," as Faulkner puts it, "with an expression almost of smiling where his teeth showed through the beard, holding his wild negroes with that one word . . . while about the wedding party the circle of faces with open mouths and torch-reflecting eyes seemed to advance and waver and shift and vanish in the smoky glare of the burning pine" he deters the mob by his mere presence (57). This Sutpen, who can stare down his own wild minions and a hostile crowd without flinching, is the "demon" Jefferson knows. Intent upon acquiring a prominent social position, he is entirely indifferent to the feeling which his actions arouse among those he wishes to join.

---

[3]Brooks, *The Yoknapatawpha Country* (New Haven: Yale University Press, 1963), 298.

With this picture of Sutpen in mind, one is surprised by the account of the demon's childhood; the child hardly seems father to the man. The boy Thomas Sutpen is above all an innocent. The son of a shiftless mountaineer, he is completely unaware of class distinctions when at the age of thirteen he arrives with his family in the Virginia Tidewater. Until his father accepts a job as a plantation hired hand, Thomas has never even seen a black or a planter. At this point he is entirely untroubled by the desire he will later feel for those trappings which will set him apart from his social inferiors.

The boy's awakening comes when he delivers a message at the Big House in which his father's employer lives. He is shocked by the doorman's curt announcement that riff-raff must come to the back door to conduct their business. For the first time Sutpen realizes that a great social chasm separates his kind from the planters above him. The boy understands the doorman's rebuff as a life-sentence to the condition of social pariah; in the sphere which the planter inhabits, he has no right even to exist.

Wounded by this discovery, Sutpen retires to the woods and contemplates what has happened to him. He is at first inclined to take the affront in the simple way of the backwoods and to shoot the man who has injured him. But gradually there comes the realization that such a response would not remove the stigma, that his rebuff at the planter's door is but one of a long series of insults that have been suffered by his family in the Tidewater, these being insults that have been delivered not so much by particular individuals as by the social system itself. So the planter whose doorman viciously snubbed Sutpen becomes an entire ruling class.

Sutpen's innocence is revealed in his decision to fight "them" with their own weapons: "[T]o combat them you have got to have what they have that made them do what the man did. You got to have land and niggers and a fine house to combat them with" (238). Sutpen's plan of revenge is nothing less than a campaign to join the class which has despised him. The irony of Sutpen's design, however, resides in the paradoxical fact that he can succeed only at the cost of becoming precisely the sort of man he hates. He intends to avenge his own rejection by becoming one who has the power to reject. Sutpen's design is innocent in its assumption that one can overcome the injustice of the class system by the simple recourse of changing one's class. His view is not only innocent but short-sighted, for, as succeeding events in *Absalom, Absalom!* will make clear, in seeking to overcome a system, Sutpen manages only to perpetuate the evil which he wants to resist.

The horror of Sutpen's design springs from the utter single-mindedness with which he pursues it and from his inability to judge the consequences of his deeds by any standard except that implicit in the plan itself. In Quentin's reconstruction of the story, Sutpen remains a flawed innocent till his death. The ruthless demon and the naive youngster are in the end one and the same because Sutpen, having at the age of fourteen lost his innocent belief that all men are equal, never overcame the deeper innocence which accepted the evaluation of human beings upon which the Southern class system rested. In short, he becomes a demon not by *violating* the ethic of his culture, but by *adopting* it.

In his only moment of self-examination which *Absalom, Absalom!* records, Sutpen asks Quentin's grandfather to point out to him the mistake which led first to Sutpen's having to repudiate his first wife and child and later to the loss of his son and heir. From the reader's perspective, and from the standpoint of Quentin and Shreve, the cold-blooded manner in which Sutpen first sets his wife aside when he discovers she has Negro blood, and then refuses to acknowledge the son of his first marriage is reprehensible. But from Sutpen's point of view, these actions are not only excusable: they are moral.

The father who gave Sutpen his daughter in marriage withheld the fact of her Negro ancestry. The son whom Sutpen cannot make his heir later endangers Sutpen's efforts to establish a dynasty by becoming engaged to his half-sister. In both cases Sutpen's design is threatened by errors for which he himself is not responsible, and therefore he feels justified in correcting them. By his own "code of logic and morality" (275) his actions are unimpeachable. But what is frightening about Sutpen is the conceptual poverty and rigidity of the moral code by which he lives. For him, human love has no value. The social contract by which the South operates—and which he has accepted—assigns worth on the basis of race and class, and no other claims are valid.

Sutpen's design, in other words, reveals the governing assumptions of Southern culture in their ugly essence. From the very beginning of his project Sutpen pledges himself to the acquisition of what his society values most: the ownership of a plantation, the possession of slaves, the manners and style of a gentleman, and a suitable wife and heir. The means by which he gains the coveted status of a planter are incidental and unimportant, and he is unconcerned with the intrinsic value of the role itself. Sutpen's only ambition is to win at the game which he feels forced to play, to be acknowledged as a master and therefore as an autonomous human being.

At this point we must ask whether Sutpen has correctly understood the nature of Southern society. Does his design effectively represent a distillation of the Southern ethic or does his innocence rather cause him to misinterpret and distort a culture which remains alien and incomprehensible to him? Sutpen's innocence has been understood as a failure to grasp the spirit of a way of life whose gestures he has learned to ape.[4] And there is in fact more than

---

[4] Brooks, *Toward Yoknapatawpha and Beyond* (New Haven: Yale University Press, 1978), 298–300.

a bit of the *nouveau riche* about him.[5] Not having been born into the planter tradition, Sutpen must attempt to create his place within it. He thus does not come by his manners naturally as does Quentin's father, for example. But, if Sutpen in one sense represents a parody of the Southern planter, he is a caricature only because he exaggerates real features of the type which in more sophisticated representatives are disguised.

The strongest indication in *Absalom, Absalom!* that Sutpen's story has a large typicality in Southern life is the fact that the Compsons, who are planters, take it seriously themselves. Although each of them has a different sort of personal investment in the figure of Sutpen, the Compson men without exception are fascinated by him, and view his case as somehow significant for the Yoknapatawpha community as a whole. Whatever the residents of Jefferson may think about Sutpen, it is an undeniable fact that he is able to assume in their midst precisely the role to which he aspires. Sutpen's Hundred and the colonel's insignia that Sutpen wears testify to the position he has won. And his victory poses a moral problem, not only for the Compsons but for their fellow townsmen, all of whom must ask themselves what Sutpen's triumph finally reveals about the community in which it occurred.

Sutpen's success is frightening because in the course of his ruthless quest he violates none of the taboos which have been designed to protect public morality. His eventual downfall is exemplary since it is caused rather than prevented by his strict adherence to the mores of his culture. It is revealing that, when Sutpen asks Quentin's grandfather to point out to him his "mistake," General Compson has nothing to say in reply. Within the social context where the question is asked, he can make no reply, for in putting away his mulatto wife and son Sutpen has done nothing of which a gentleman of the time need be ashamed. Similarly, Sutpen's virtually outright theft of land from the Indians (the questionable business deal which establishes his fortune) and his brutal wrestling matches with his savage West Indian Negroes fall within the bounds of accepted male behavior. Though Sutpen's rise to power is more sudden and graceless than the ascent of the Compsons has been, its essential form is no different. Sutpen's single-mindedness simply makes the lines of development more distinct.

The collapse of Sutpen's empire is as revealing as its conquest. Although a full treatment of this topic must await our discussion of Sutpen's progeny, it is clear that what brings him down is the inability of his design to accommodate the human need for love. But, here again, the fault in Sutpen's design reflects the cultural ethic it mirrors.

---

[5]Michael Millgate, *The Achievement of William Faulkner* (Lincoln: University of Nebraska Press, 1978), 159.

Sutpen's son Charles Bon rises up against him because his father refuses to acknowledge him. But if, as the narrators surmise, Bon is indeed a mulatto, then within the context of Southern culture Sutpen is under no ethical obligation to recognize Bon as his offspring. The unspoken rule in the antebellum South was that the white master was permitted to take a slave as his mistress so long as he did so discreetly; any resulting children assumed their places among the rest of the slave offspring. A mulatto child had no legal claim on its white father, and the notion that a Negro might become a legitimate member of a white family was simply unthinkable. By refusing to acknowledge Bon, then, Sutpen is following rather than transgressing a social taboo.

Nevertheless Sutpen's refusal to recognize his son as his own abrogates the filial bond which should exist between them. Sutpen's action is ironic on several counts, not only because his immoral act proceeds from a putatively moral commitment, but also because the outcast Bon is far more refined than either his father or his white brother. Sutpen himself apparently feels no remorse over the fate of his Absalom; however, for the reader, Bon's plight is all the more pathetic because in addition to his Sutpen blood, Bon has gained all of the social attainments which should grant him a place of honor in the family household. The only obstacle between Bon and his father is the intrinsically insignificant—and except to Sutpen, undiscovered—trace of Negro blood in his son. According to the logic of Sutpen's design and the racist social ethic it mirrors, however, that taint is fully sufficient to justify Charles Bon's disinheritance.

Bon's decision to marry his sister and so to force his father to acknowledge him pits the force of human love against the iron strictures of Sutpen's design. Bon enlists the incestuous love of sister for brother in his struggle against Sutpen's code in order to counter the taboo which forbids Sutpen to acknowledge his son. Because of his blind adherence to his design Sutpen refuses to speak the word which would establish the rightful bond and would forbid the illicit one, and thus in the end both family and design come crashing down. The collapse of Sutpen's house is the result of an internal flaw in his design which is in turn a reflection of the corrupt ethic of the larger culture. In maintaining the racial taboo which thwarts legitimate familial love Sutpen opens the door to chaotic emotional forces which destroy the social fabric the taboo is meant to protect.

The tragedy of Sutpen's family is thus a parable which speaks of the spiritual corruption at the heart of Southern culture, and Quentin is thoroughly justified in telling the tale as an explanation of his region. Although in many ways anomalous, Sutpen's case is instructive precisely because the elements of the Southern ethos that it exaggerates are those which society has every reason to disguise. Sutpen is indeed reductively single-minded and obsessive in pursuing his design, as established planters of the Compson variety are not.

But the logic of the code which Sutpen so fiercely applies is simply the ethic of Southern culture reduced to its awful essentials. He has stripped away the façade of gentility which all too often masks the dehumanizing power of the Southern system. Sutpen is not a misfit who has disregarded the spirit of his society in favor of the cruel letter of its law, but a *naif* who in adopting the ethic of his culture in its simplest form reveals its true nature.

IV

In addition to the evidence to be found within the text for regarding Sutpen's story as representative of the flaw at the heart of Southern culture, there are external reasons for so regarding it. The pattern which Sutpen follows in rising from the ranks of the white yeoman to the planter class is one which historians have since confirmed as typical.[6] The large majority of slaveholders and cotton growers in the South at the time of the Civil War were men who had previously left meager farms in older, better established regions for virgin land which could be turned into cotton fields. Such men prospered by dint of hard work (and of course a booming cotton market), and when they grew rich they sought to adopt the airs of the English country gentry. Embarrassingly few even of the older families who had originally settled the coasts of Virginia and South Carolina could legitimately claim kinship with noble families in Europe, and virtually none of the new cotton barons had warrant for boasting of such connections. The Cavalier legend which assigned to the younger sons of adventurous European nobles the rich plantations of the South had very little historical substance. What in fact happened was that the planter class embraced the Cavalier myth as a way of legitimizing its power.

Poorly educated, uncertain of the permanence of his newly-acquired wealth, defensive concerning the institution of slavery, the typical antebellum planter donned the cloak of gentility in order to disguise his anxieties beneath the cover of respected tradition. These apprehensive *nouveaux riches* often fell victim to their own deceptions. The bogus genealogies and pompous rhetoric so characteristic of the time are testimony to the lengths to which Southern planters went in order to invent for themselves noble origins, and thus they speak all the more powerfully of the sense of illegitimacy such pretensions sought to mask.

The startling contrast between Sutpen as he sits at the head of his mahogany table under an imported crystal chandelier and the naked demon who

---

[6] W.J. Cash was one of the first to make much of this fact, in *The Mind of the South* (New York: Alfred Knopf, 1941); it has become a commonplace among students of Southern history. See, for a recent example, Daniel Joseph Singal, *The War Within* (Chapel Hill: University of North Carolina Press, 1982).

wrestles slaves in a torch-lit barn is a pictorial representation of an equally sharp dichotomy within the Southern mind. The saga of Sutpen's rise to power is, in effect, a history in miniature of the planter class; Faulkner has here reformulated the myth of the founder. In place of the old myth of the Cavalier, Faulkner offers the new saga of the ruthless innocent. Sutpen's story is thus a crucial element in Faulkner's indictment of the South, and it exposes the illusion on which the self-understanding of the culture rests.

Faulkner's new myth takes the following form. Those who established the social order which gave birth to Southern culture were motivated by a lust for power. Fugitives, for whatever reason, from older societies in which they were victims, they entered a virgin land where it was possible for them to make themselves masters. They conquered the land, and the more ambitious and industrious among them did indeed become a landed oligarchy. But the new society these fugitives and opportunists created mirrored the power structures from which they had fled. The South developed a class system based on race and property which was every bit as oppressive as those regimes from which its founders had escaped. In order to hide this fact both from themselves and from the world, Southerners constructed a mask of innocent gentility. Those who had gained their wealth and status by means of exploiting others claimed that what they had acquired was in fact theirs by long-established divine right. They thus acted in accordance with a romance built along the lines of the Gothic fiction which they so often deeply admired. The planter oligarchy claimed to hold its position by virtue of noble lineage and adherence to the rules of chivalry. But this romance was, quite simply, a cultural illusion.

Faulkner's new historical myth, which first takes shape in *Absalom, Absalom!*, thus has the dual effect of exposing the romance of innocence as illusion, and of establishing a revisionist narrative of the founding of Southern culture. The story of Sutpen's empire replaces the bankrupt myth of the Cavalier. In *Absalom, Absalom!*, the romance of innocence comes to have a double meaning. Sutpen's faith in Southern values is naive because that ethic legitimates the very exploitation against which he rebels; but his own account of his actions seeks nevertheless to present them as blameless. The romance of innocence is thus a fallacious defense of a culture which actually believes its own lies about itself—and is well served by that hard-won belief.

In mounting his indictment of the Cavalier myth of the founder, Faulkner could draw in some measure on the evidence presented by his own great-grandfather's novel, W.C. Falkner's famous romance *The White Rose of Memphis*.[7] Sutpen indeed has much in common with Old Colonel Falkner

---

[7] William C. Falkner, *The White Rose of Memphis* with an introduction by Robert Cantwell (New York: Coley Taylor, 1953; first published, 1881).

himself. Both arrive in northern Mississippi in the second quarter of the nineteenth century with no money and no connections, and bearing the faint stigma of past scandal. Each succeeds in establishing family and fortune despite the hostility of a substantial portion of the community. Both men are ruthless empire-builders who are first elected Confederate colonels by their men and then rejected for reckless behavior on the field of battle. W.C. Falkner, like Sutpen, is finally killed by a disaffected associate whom he has apparently cheated in some way.[8]

Sutpen's history is thus an extension of the legend of the Old Colonel, which loomed very large in Faulkner's imagination. More important than the parallels between his fictional character and his great-grandfather are the parallels between the apologies each makes for the apparently heinous deeds which lead in each case to worldly success. Sutpen insists on the integrity of his design; W.C. Falkner defends himself by writing a fictionalized account of his own youth in which the hero manages to prove his innocence in the face of charges of murder and bigamy. In each case the figure whom the community takes to be a demon defends himself by asserting his complete compliance with cultural standards. Each maintains that the appearance of culpability is the result of unfortunate circumstances which obscure what are in fact entirely honorable actions. Sutpen does put his first wife aside, but only when he discovers her Negro ancestry, and he is therefore within the rights which any Southerner would acknowledge. W.C. Falkner kills a rival, but only when challenged and therefore honor-bound to defend himself. Edward Demar (the elder Falkner's fictional alter ego) goes to the length of laying his crimes at the door of a double, and thus his guilt becomes entirely a matter of appearance. In each case, the defense of the energetic and envied man amounts to a reinterpretation of his actions as those of a gentleman living by the code of honor which regulates his society.

The moral irony of this sort of apology is that it counters the alleged values of the society to which it is directed with the actual ethic by which it operates. Bigamy is wrong—except when one of one's spouses is black and the other white. Murder is forbidden except when one's honor is at stake. Racism and the code of honor are at odds with the alleged value of respect for all persons, and it is to the former rather than the latter standards that Southern society is actually committed. The romance which allows such characters to transform their misdeeds into the prerogatives of a gentleman suggests in miniature the aristocratic illusion with which their society veils its *modus operandi*. The theme of innocence is thus common to both the founders of

---

[8] I have drawn here on the first chapter of Judith Wittenburg's *Faulkner: The Transfiguration of Biography* (Lincoln: University of Nebraska Press, 1979) as well as the biographies written by Blotner and Minter.

the Southern order and the culture which is their legacy. Southern society actually believes the romance which it has fabricated in order to justify the design of exploitation which it has in fact carried out. What W.J. Cash calls "the mind of the South" is innocent in exactly Sutpen's double sense. Though its apology for its existence is a fallacious romanticization of exploitation, Southerners still believe the romance to be true; they innocently accept the protest of moral innocence.

Faulkner himself, unlike his great-grandfather, and Quentin, unlike Sutpen, are troubled by the moral defectiveness of the romance by which the South has sought to justify itself. And it is to Quentin that we now turn in order to assess Faulkner's revisions of the cherished traditional myth of the founder.

V

Quentin Compson's interest in Sutpen is, as we have noted, intensely personal. The fact that Quentin compulsively relates the Sutpen saga to his Harvard roommate only a few months before his own suicide is reason enough to believe that Quentin sees a connection between the collapse of this neighboring planter family and the impending demise of his own. Critics have long noted that it is Quentin who introduces the theme of incest into the reconstruction of Sutpen's history and that, when he and Shreve take over as narrators, Sutpen's sons play a larger role than they play earlier in the novel. For these reasons we can hardly doubt that Quentin projects his situation onto the stage that the Sutpens occupy in his imagination. It would be a mistake, however, to interpret Quentin's interest in Sutpen's Hundred in purely psychological terms. His preoccupation with the Sutpens, like his obsession with his sister in *The Sound and the Fury,* is an integral part of his attempt to make sense of the class and culture for which he has inherited responsibility. Quentin identifies himself with Henry Sutpen and Charles Bon not only because, like him, they fail to measure up to the expectations of their father and pretend to be in love with a doomed sister, but because their tragedy exposes the flaw which is slowly unraveling the fabric of their entire social order. If the story of Sutpen represents a revisionist myth of the Southern founder, the problem facing Bon and Henry (and by implication Quentin) is how to confront the moral and psychological consequences of the foundation which Sutpen has laid.

As Quentin constructs it, the history of the Sutpens of Yoknapatawpha can be summarized as follows: Sutpen succeeds in establishing a plantation, and consolidates his position in the community by marrying the daughter of a respected Methodist merchant. The marriage produces two children, Henry and Judith. Judith is something of a hoyden and is fascinated by her father's brutal pastimes; Henry by contrast is shy and is intimidated by his father. When

Henry matriculates at the state university, he is befriended by an older, more worldly student who proves to be Sutpen's son by his first wife. Henry brings Charles Bon to Sutpen's Hundred, where Judith, ignorant of his relation to her, falls in love with him. Bon eventually reciprocates her feelings, and they subsequently become engaged. Bon then discovers that Sutpen is in all likelihood his father, but continues his courtship of Judith even so, in the hope of forcing Sutpen to acknowledge him.

The Civil War intervenes, and Sutpen and his sons go off to join the conflict. During the course of the war, Sutpen and Henry meet (Henry having by now learned that Bon is his brother). Though Sutpen acknowledges to Henry that Bon is his son and that Bon has black blood, he yet refuses to confront Bon himself, who has decided to return to Mississippi and marry Judith. Henry rides with him, hoping all the while that Bon will change his mind. But Bon remains adamant, and at the gate of Sutpen's Hundred, Henry shoots and kills him, and then flees.

After the war, Sutpen returns and attempts to salvage the wreckage of his design. His wife has died during the war, and so he offers to marry her sister Rosa, but only on the condition that she demonstrate her fertility by first conceiving for him a son. The outraged Rosa refuses, and in a last desperate attempt to produce a male heir, Sutpen seduces the granddaughter of his white tenant. She, however, gives birth to a girl, and Sutpen repudiates the liaison whereupon her grandfather, Wash Jones, kills Sutpen with a scythe in retaliation.

Judith and her mulatto sister Clytemnestra continue to live in the decaying Sutpen mansion. They become the guardians of Bon's mulatto son by a morganatic marriage, and, later, of Bon's grandson Jim Bond. Both men live lives of bitter isolation; the latter at last leaves Mississippi and is never heard from again. Henry, the lone remaining male descendent of Thomas Sutpen, finally returns to Sutpen's Hundred, where Quentin and Miss Rosa discover him in June, 1909. Quentin sees and, presumably, talks to Henry on that occasion. In December of that year, Rosa returns to remove the now decrepit Henry to a place where he can receive medical attention, but Clytie sets fire to the house to forestall Henry's removal, and all that remains of Sutpen's design—the rotting house and the wasted heir—perishes in the flames.

This tale, as I have reconstructed it from the disjointed speculations of Quentin and Shreve (and any coherent version of the history can only be a reconstruction of events reported through fictional hearsay), is a narrative of decline. It chronicles the demise of a great house in a way reminiscent of Greek tragedy—of the *Oresteia* for example. In the case of the Sutpens, the curse which brings about the catastrophe is the sign of Thomas Sutpen's innocent belief in his design. He develops an obsessive single-mindedness which causes him, with disastrous results, to ignore the universal demands of familial love.

Faulkner here uses the striking case of paternal rejection of a son to suggest the power of a racist social hierarchy to disrupt primary social bonds. Discarded sons are rare; but casual, unthinking brutality is, in this society, very common indeed. By allowing the rejection he meets with at the door of a Virginia aristocrat to commit him to an absolute principle of revenge, Sutpen sets in motion a chain of events which results in the destruction of his entire family.

Quentin's version of the tragedy focuses on the catastrophic effects of Sutpen's revenge on his progeny. Sutpen's children are set against one another by their father's refusal to acknowledge his eldest son. And Quentin's contribution to the reconstruction of the saga is the introduction of the themes of incest and miscegenation into the general design of the revenge-plot.

Sutpen's original purposes are threatened when he discovers that his first wife is of Negro ancestry. He deals with this difficulty by setting aside his first family and starting a new one. However, the threat reappears when the tainted son is introduced into the new, legitimate family. By refusing to acknowledge Bon as his son, Sutpen has unwittingly repeated the offense of the Virginia planter who inspired his own design of revenge. The difference, of course, is that Sutpen is motivated by the cultural taboo against miscegenation. And the rejected Bon retaliates in kind by threatening to break the incest taboo in order to win recognition from his father.

Judith and Henry finally become pawns in this struggle between father and eldest son. Sutpen and Bon allow Judith to fall in love with a man whom she does not know to be her brother. Henry, likewise, develops a strangely erotic dependence on Bon.[9] But Henry's love for sister and father and his sense of honor do at last overpower his attraction to Bon, for in the end he takes Bon's life. Moreover, Henry and Judith, traumatized as rudely by the near fruition of the threatened incestuous union as by the actual fratricide, subsequently withdraw from the world beyond the family, and in the end both die childless. Sutpen, now an old man, and lacking the vigor to match his ambition, is killed in a last feeble attempt to establish a new line after his first children have effectively destroyed each other. Sutpen's progeny in effect manage ultimately to destroy their father's dream by refusing to continue the line of descent which is crucial to his design.

The importance of the theme of incest for an understanding of the psychology of the Sutpens by far transcends its use as a weapon in Bon's war against his father. For all the family relationships are incestuous in the sense that no member of the family is free to establish a meaningful union beyond the family circle while the cycle of revenge remains in motion. The Sutpens

---

[9]See the passage on p. 108, *Absalom, Absalom!*. See also King's commentary in *A Southern Renaissance,* 122.

become an insular unit which is self-enclosed because, in the game which they are playing, the emotional stakes are so high that all have too much invested to leave it. Bon's sense of identity finally depends upon his father's recognition; Henry cannot be sure of the status of his relation either to his father or his sister while the status of his elder brother remains in question; Judith's attempt to leave the family circle by marrying is thwarted in an even crueler way when her lover turns out to be her brother. And this larger incestuous context is complicated by the process of doubling that it engenders.

We have already noted the strange attraction that Henry and Bon feel for each other even before they discover that they are brothers. Part of the fascination which Henry feels is simply that of a young provincial for a man of the world. And we may assume that Bon in turn takes pleasure in molding the tastes of so eager a student. However, the psychology of these two men, as it is constructed by the narrators, suggests that their attraction for each other runs far deeper than the sort of easy camaraderie which they initially seem to share.

The childhood episode which the narrators find to be most revealing of Henry's nature is the occasion on which he hides in a hayloft and watches his father wrestle with one of his West Indian slaves. Henry is repelled by the violence, and the men who have gathered for the spectacle find him vomiting in disgust. He has, in other words, something of his mother's moral fastidiousness, and, throughout his life, Henry unsuccessfully struggles to accommodate the Sutpen demand for male assertiveness with his Coldfield sense of propriety.

Charles Bon, on the other hand, is almost entirely free of compunction. He radiates a sort of self-assured nonchalance which Henry envies. And, while Henry remains a virgin—at least until Bon takes him to visit New Orleans—Bon has kept an octoroon mistress since reaching manhood. Bon lives a life devoted entirely to the cultivation of the senses; he acknowledges no moral barrier except an elaborate code of manners which is exclusively designed to preserve the appearance of honor. The only matter about which Bon exhibits even the slightest anxiety is the identity of his father.

In short, the relationship between Henry and Bon is one which involves their being in effect aspects of a single identity. Henry is the "light" twin, the legitimate son who scrupulously obeys the rules; Bon is the dark twin, the bastard who knows no rules and gives rein to his passions without hesitation.

Bon's announced intention to marry his sister draws the sibling circle even more tightly together. Henry and Judith share from childhood a bond so strong that they can almost be called twins but they are complementary rather than similar in character. In the barn scene to which I have already alluded, Judith is present as well, and, while Henry is shocked by the brutal display, Judith is attracted, almost mesmerized. Whereas Judith longs to emulate her father,

Henry resembles his mother, despite his efforts to break free of this disposition. The complicity between Henry and Judith reaches its height when Judith comes to love the man who has been the love of Henry's life.

After Henry discovers that Bon is his brother a kind of perverted love triangle arises in which each of the siblings in turn competes against one of the others in order to win the love of a third. Thus Henry's love for his friend and brother Bon works to undercut his love for his sister, whom Bon would destroy were he to marry her. Bon in turn pits his love for Judith against his love for Henry, knowing that by continuing his engagement to Judith he is forcing Henry to choose between them. And Judith knows that, if she agrees to marry Bon, she will cut herself off forever from Henry.

The involuted and divisive loves between the siblings are, of course, rooted in their relations to their father. Bon insists on marrying Judith in order to wrench from Sutpen recognition of their familial relationship. Henry and Judith, forced to choose between love for each other and love for Bon, are also forced to choose between love for their father and love for their errant elder brother. Sutpen clearly hopes to coerce Henry and Judith into rejecting Bon as he has done. And by using his legitimate children to ostracize the bastard, Sutpen in effect enrolls them in his design: if Henry and Judith turn Bon away, they will do so for the sake of the family honor, just as Sutpen has done before them.

It is significant, however, that, while Bon and Judith are strong-willed enough to carry out their plan to marry regardless of the consequences, it is Henry who in the end acts to prevent them from doing so. Bon and Judith are most similar to their father in their Sutpen-like rebellion against him; Henry is least like him in obeying him. At one level Sutpen succeeds in coercing his children to participate in his design. The "false" claimant to Sutpen's acknowledgment is killed by the rightful heir. But in slaying his brother, Henry repudiates his father in a different sense. Thus Henry turns obedience into rebellion by following Sutpen's wishes—and then forsaking Sutpen's house. Henry's decision to obey his father is also a rejection of Sutpen's design. In killing Bon, Henry has already seized the fate which will reach sad completion forty-four years later when he is burned alive in the decayed remains of the Sutpen mansion. Henry destroys himself to lift the curse which his father began.

Henry's long assessment of his dilemma, as he weighs the respective consequences of allowing Bon to marry Judith and shooting him, is the ethical center of *Absalom, Absalom!*. In killing Bon, Henry performs the act of paradoxical moral heroism which demonstrates that it is he rather than Sutpen who is the true tragic hero of the work. For Sutpen, as we have seen, is an innocent who is incapable of moral distinctions, and who has unthinkingly accepted the code and logic which have brought about precisely the dilemma

Henry faces. Sutpen's one recorded ethical act is moral acceptance of a fundamentally unethical system. Placed as he is in the struggle between his father and his brother, Henry is forced to see the inadequacy of Sutpen's code. He cannot treat his friend and brother as slave, although, since Bon is a Negro by the South's manner of reckoning, the ethic of Henry's culture demands that he do so. Yet neither can Henry allow his brother and sister to consummate an incestuous union. Henry is faced with an impossible choice: to countenance fratricide or incest. He chooses fratricide, but in so doing he also opts for a kind of suicide. Since no truly ethical option is open to him, he settles upon a course of action which will destroy the immoral context itself. In less abstract terms, the evil which infects his family is so deep that the only cure for it is the family's destruction.

In making the tragic choice which is the moral climax of *Absalom, Absalom!*, Henry follows the example of his maternal grandfather. We have seen how Henry is in many ways the least Sutpen-like of the siblings; what most profoundly sets him apart is the scrupulousness which he inherits from his Coldfield mother. The only real alternative to the Sutpen code to be found within the novel is the distorted Puritanism in accordance with which Henry's grandfather, alone of all the citizens of Jefferson, concludes that the Southern cause in the Civil War is morally insupportable.

Coldfield's objection to the war is that it is mounted in defense of an economic system built upon "opportunism and brigandage" rather than upon "stern morality." A devout man himself, he envisions man's relationship to God as a contractual agreement whereby an honest life accumulates a favorable balance of merit in heaven. The human order should reflect the divine, and, so far as Coldfield is concerned, any society which rewards exploitation deserves destruction. He thus abhors the Civil War on the one hand as a waste of the goods which God has entrusted to Southerners, and welcomes it on the other as a just punishment of a sinful people. He registers his protest against the South by refusing to sell goods to the army and by sealing himself in his attic, where he slowly starves to death.

But the Coldfield code, too, is flawed, for in one sense it is simply an inversion of Sutpen morality. Like Sutpen, Coldfield insists on a reductive scheme of absolutes which has no place for love. He treats his daughter Rosa, for example, with a harshness equal to Sutpen's. In his obsession with his spiritual accounts he is oblivious to her welfare. But Coldfield's Puritanism differs from Sutpen's ethic of power in that it includes an allegiance to God which takes precedence over any social structure. Coldfield is able not only to condemn his society but to renounce his own earthly well-being in the light of what he takes to be the demands of a righteous God. Thus, while Coldfield's ethic is seriously deficient, it still gives him a point of reference from which to judge the corrupt code of the Southern planter which Sutpen has adopted.

Henry's renunciation of his patrimony takes a form reminiscent of his grandfather's act of moral defiance. Having seen that Sutpen's design is unalterably corrupt—and that he is party to its corruption—he repudiates it altogether. He lacks the spiritual resources which would be necessary to redeem his family, but he is able to discern its sin. Unlike Coldfield's, Henry's action is more than symbolic; but, like his grandfather, Henry ends his life in a secluded attic, forgotten by the community which he has renounced. While his sacrifice is destructive rather than redemptive, what it destroys is a terrible evil.

Henry's decision, then, is a reversal of Sutpen's original commitment to his design. Stung by the class system, the elder Sutpen plotted a scheme of revenge against it, and took as his goal the attainment of a position of mastery and power. But, when Henry kills his brother and renounces his patrimony, he does so to put an end to Sutpen's cycle of revenge and to repudiate his claims to power. Within a design committed to arbitrary structures of power where human love is forced into distorted shapes, the only ethical action is one that seeks to dismantle the design itself. As the first Sutpen who is not "innocent," Henry must take the guilt of the family on himself in order to remove the Sutpen curse.

Judith also pays penance for the sins of her father and older brother. After the death of her fiancé, she lives a life of unselfish seclusion, caring first for her impoverished father and then for Bon's orphaned mulatto son. In the long denouement of the tragedy that has had its climax in Henry's murder of his brother, Judith uncomplainingly sacrifices herself to the comfort of those doomed by Sutpen's curse. She thus becomes the embodiment of Sutpen courage turned to the service of love. Although she is little more than a pawn in the struggle between her father and brothers, Judith yet represents a motherly kind of solicitude toward the men of the household after Bon's death. Henry kills in the name of love and honor, but it is she who cares for the dying. By choosing the life of a widow she renounces her own role in Sutpen's design, and by remaining to minister to the victims of the Sutpen curse she alone is able to embody genuine faithfulness and love.

Henry's decision to repudiate Sutpen's design and Judith's penitential life of self-sacrificing service break the grip of Sutpen's curse on his progeny. Once the cruel reality of the power ethic is revealed beneath the veil of planter gentility, Sutpen's children can no longer reconcile the caste system with the notion of honor it purports to express. They are forced therefore to destroy Sutpen's design in the name of those virtues which the design is supposed to embody. Sutpen conceives his design in order to establish himself and his family as masters; instead, it gives rise to a situation in which his children are unable to acknowledge either fraternal or filial bonds, and so must rise up against their father. Since within the structures which Sutpen has accepted it is impossible to give or to receive love in legitimate ways, the only loving action open to his children is the destruction of the design itself. Sutpen's innocence prevents his recognition of the immorality of his professed moral code, but Henry and Judith are so placed that such naiveté is impossible: the price of Sutpen's innocence is moral tragedy for his children.

VI

Absalom, Absalom!, like *The Sound and the Fury*, is thus an indictment of the moral corruption lying at the heart of Southern culture. Sutpen's story is, in revisionist form, another myth of the founder, proposing in effect that Southern society was established upon a basis of exploitation which the "official" myth cannot conceal. Caddy's fall and the speciousness of the feminine ideal in *The Sound and the Fury* find in *Absalom, Absalom!* a kind of counterpoint in the ruthless innocence of the male type as it is quintessentially expressed in Sutpen. For Quentin and for Henry, neither of whom is able to break free from the corrupt social order which he has inherited, the only action possible once the veil of innocence has been removed is the great negative of suicide. These two novels stand not only as stirring literary explorations of the themes of incest and revenge, but as spiritual parables of a culture on the verge of self-destruction.

Faulkner's indictment of Southern culture moves from a depiction of present decay to an examination of the source of that corruption in the false innocence of its founders. His new historical myth of the founder serves to explain within the framework of a narrative the hidden dynamics of a culture which has become a mystery to itself. For Quentin, as for Faulkner, the story remains fragmented and incomplete. The pattern that emerges from *Absalom, Absalom!* is one of decline and pending collapse. The only sense that either Quentin or his creator can make of his culture resides in a recognition that its original categories of self-understanding are flawed; the only responsible action which one who has accepted its highest values can undertake is quite simply to repudiate it. Quentin's despair over his sister in *The Sound and the Fury* is in *Absalom, Absalom!* extended to his entire culture.

But though Quentin's struggle to make moral sense of his tradition comes to an end in *Absalom, Absalom!*, Faulkner's parallel struggle does not. The historical myth which he had developed in this novel had already brought within his purview an aspect of his culture which he had yet fully to explore. We have seen how Henry, the real tragic hero of the Sutpen saga, is able to transcend the ethic of power by drawing upon his Coldfield Puritan heritage. Miss Rosa Coldfield begins her denunciation of Sutpen by claiming that he has violated the divine charter which gave him and his kind the right to establish a new order on the virgin soil of the South. Implicit in this claim is the belief that any full explanation of the South's demise must begin with an account of the religious warrant by which it justifies its existence.

Sutpen's fall is the result of his innocence. But his is an innocence of a curious kind. His naiveté finally entails a radical misconception of reality. His determination to live according to an exploitative code bends the force of love back upon itself until it destroys his design. By ignoring the need for love which his desire for acknowledgment distorts, he creates a hell for himself and his progeny. The curse which Sutpen unleashes is the judgment of those ultimate powers which he has ignored. The morality of the Coldfields which enables Henry to renounce his tainted patrimony understands at least this much. But, clearly, for Faulkner there is no more room for love in the stern moralism of Southern Puritanism than there is in the ethic of exploitation which it condemns. The religious perspective which Faulkner and his narrators bring to bear upon the Sutpen story is finally inadequate to the task of explaining the true nature of the love which is distorted by Sutpen's design. In both *The Sound and the Fury* and *Absalom, Absalom!* Faulkner senses that only a religious assessment will sufficiently account for the tragedy he depicts, but in each case he finds the theological schemes available to him woefully inadequate to the task at hand.

In order to complete his new historical myth he had also to reinterpret the religious myth by which the South understands its relation to ultimate reality. And this is the enterprise which he began in his next great Yoknapatawpha novel, *Light in August*.

Chapter 3

A PURITAN INDICTMENT: MYTH VS. IRONY IN *LIGHT IN AUGUST*

I

In *Light in August,* Faulkner attempts for the first time a thorough-going examination of explicitly religious practice and belief within the Southern context. As we have seen, the shape of Faulkner's critique in *Absalom, Absalom!* seems necessarily to imply that the corrupt ethical standards of the South are rooted in assumptions about the meaning of life so deep as to require to be thought of as essentially religious. But it is only when he comes to write the tale of Joe Christmas and Lena Grove that he begins to explore the direct expressions of religious conviction in the life of Yoknapatawpha County. For this reason, though *Light in August* is an earlier work than *Absalom, Absalom!*, it serves, in a certain sense, as a commentary upon the Sutpen saga.

Indeed, the two novels were begun within the space of three years, and, oddly enough, both bore the working title of *Dark House*.[1] It is not surprising, therefore, that they take parallel directions. In the first draft of *Light in August* Gail Hightower is the central character, and the "dark house" of the original title refers to the "man-stale" dwelling to which he has retreated after losing his pulpit. The "dark house" of what would finally see print as *Absalom, Absalom!* is of course the Sutpen mansion. In both cases, however,

---

[1] Blotner, Vol. 1, 701–702; 828–30.

despite the difference of putative subject, the action of the novel involves the demise of the Southern aristocratic tradition and dramatizes the tension between the code of the Cavalier and the morality of the Puritan. In the course of writing *Absalom, Absalom!*, Faulkner chose to concentrate on the Cavalier tradition as represented by Thomas Sutpen; in *Light in August* he concentrates upon the Puritan ethic which Sutpen flouts. But the two codes are closely related, even if they exemplify conflicting strains within the harmony of the culture at large, and *Light in August* may be understood as a full exploration of the "Coldfield morality" which, with Henry as its principal agent, stands in a contrapuntal relation to the desires of Sutpen's plan.[2]

By keeping in mind the point of departure which these two novels share, we find the basis for an answer to a question which has long vexed Faulkner's readers: what is the role of Gail Hightower within the otherwise symmetrical interweaving of the comic tale of Lena Grove with the tragic story of Joe Christmas?[3] Hightower, we may say, represents Faulkner's attempt to find common ground between the traditions of Cavalier and Puritan, and thus to render a picture of the whole of white Southern society. Through him Faulkner seeks to demonstrate that, although these two traditions stand in ethical opposition to each other (as *Absalom, Absalom!* indeed makes clear), they share a fundamental moral sterility. Neither as a Calvinist preacher nor as an heir of the Cavaliers does Hightower prove capable of saving the victim of racism or of responding to feminine love.

Hightower represents, in effect, a less fully realized Quentin Compson, a character who finds himself unable to sustain his dreams of ancestral glory in the face of practical ethical problems with which he is not prepared to deal. Just as Quentin is trapped by the past and by a wooden moral code which prevents him from accepting his sister's impassioned sexuality, so Hightower is unable to enter the natural cycle of love and birth as it unfolds in the story of Lena Grove, and proves impotent in his attempt to prevent the tragedy which overtakes Joe Christmas in his own house. While Hightower, unlike Quentin, attempts to break out of the prison of self-consciousness and of obsession with the past, he finally lapses into the sort of defeated self-absorption which brought him to Jefferson in the first place.[4]

The figure of Hightower serves as a thematic link connecting *Light in August* to *Absalom, Absalom!* and indeed to *The Sound and the Fury* in Faulkner's indictment of Southern culture, but it is by no means the only such parallel. The "Presbyterian hell" to which Quentin wishes to banish both

---

[2]*Vide* Blotner, Vol. 1, 701–702; Minter, 23, 129, 153–54.
[3]*Vide* Millgate, *The Achievement of William Faulkner*, 130, and Alfred Kazin, "The Stillness of *Light in August*," in *Three Decades of Criticism*, 256.
[4]King, *A Southern Renaissance*, 84–85.

himself and Caddy, and the "Coldfield morality" which Henry Sutpen turns on his father both find an even fuller expression in the story of Joe Christmas. Though it figures in one guise or another in each of the Yoknapatawpha novels, it is indeed in *Light in August* that Faulkner presents his most careful and most searching account of Puritan sensibility.

The fact that Faulkner here focuses upon the Southern white yeoman class lends to this novel a tone different from that characterizing *The Sound and the Fury* and *Absalom, Absalom!*. Alfred Kazin accordingly complains that the novel is "written down," that Faulkner, like the fictional Hightower, is never able fully to enter into the lives of the characters whom he observes.[5] But Faulkner's detachment paradoxically enriches his work in other ways. It enables him to treat the story of Lena Grove as pure pastoral despite the dark circumstances of her journey, and it allows him to describe the dynamics of Christmas's tragedy with a ruthless completeness which is in the end more satisfying than the brilliant ambiguity of *The Sound and the Fury* and *Absalom, Absalom!*. On the scale of his emotional involvement with his work, *Light in August* stands somewhere between *As I Lay Dying,* which Faulkner himself accurately described as a *tour de force* and *The Sound and the Fury*, which he always regarded as his most unambiguously personal novel.[6]

But though the difference in social milieu between the world of the Compson novels and the yeoman setting of *Light in August* may explain the pervasive difference in tone which we have noted, it does not explain why Faulkner has joined the stories of Joe Christmas and Lena Grove. The relation between these two strands of his narrative constitutes a thematic and structural puzzle. Unlike the four sections of *The Sound and the Fury,* each of which attempts to make sense of Caddy's behavior, or the various efforts in *Absalom, Absalom!* to determine the cause of Sutpen's downfall, the separate strands of this novel seem barely related at all. Not only do Lena Grove and Joe Christmas never encounter each other; with the exception of Lucas Burch, they seem not even to share any common acquaintances. Furthermore, Lena's tale is pastoral and comic, while Joe's is grimly tragic.

Light in August in fact reveals a fundamental separation between what one might term the "mythic" and "ironic" modes characteristic of Faulkner's art, which in this novel belong to different fictional contexts altogether. Both forms of expression serve Faulkner's ongoing attempt to indict and escape restrictive Southern patterns of thought, but the mythic mode tends in the direction of escape, and the ironic in that of indictment. We have seen how in

---

[5]Kazin, "The Stillness of *Light in August*," 263.
[6]Faulkner makes this claim about *As I Lay Dying* and *The Sound and the Fury* in his interview with Cynthia Grenier, *Lion in the Garden,* Meriwether and Millgate, eds. (Lincoln, Nebraska: University of Nebraska Press, 1980), 118.

The Sound and the Fury Faulkner seeks on the one hand to condemn a decayed aristocratic tradition, while on the other he is able to construct from the debris of its collapse a timeless work of art which is a compensatory source of consolation to him. The central figure of the novel is Caddy, but she herself is revealed to us in both modes. To Benjy she represents the nurturing mother and a sympathetic nature ("Caddy smelled like trees"), while to Jason she exemplifies whorish and domineering female rapacity. Quentin, who must reconcile his love for his sister with his desire to preserve the code of honor, is torn by these contradictory feelings. Dilsey alone is able through her Christian faith to accept Caddy as a sinful human being who is neither the potential savior of her family nor the demon who destroyed it; but such spontaneous, unanalyzed faith is inaccessible either to the jaded Compsons or to their sophisticated creator.

A similar dialectic is at work in *Absalom, Absalom!*, where Faulkner plays on the myth of the Southern founder to make of Thomas Sutpen a "giant in the earth," but then effectively shatters that myth by exposing Sutpen's fatal "innocence." The myth in which Sutpen seeks to clothe himself is, like the robes which Benjy and Quentin attempt to hang on Caddy, not cut to fit the living human being. The ironic contrast between history and myth, man and costume, disrupts the masquerade. Caddy and Sutpen are tragic in large part because the roles in which society has cast them are false; that is to say, these roles preclude the full expression of their human complexity. Caddy is betrayed by the Southern feminine ideal because that ideal denies female sexuality. Sutpen falls because the ideal of the founder prevents him from expressing paternal love.

What is lacking in Faulkner's ambivalent treatment of his culture is a middle term which would allow him to accommodate the human need for an ideal to the day-to-day realities of human existence. Faulkner expresses his overriding sense of the necessity for a new sort of myth by substituting his own "Tyrrhenian vase" for the broken ideals of the Southern lady and the Southern founder. The works of art which are the novels themselves not only transform but finally seek to replace the sordid reality which they describe, and thus in one sense replace the ideals they destroy. Yet for this very reason they fail in some measure to capture, and so fail to elevate, the density of human existence itself. Faulkner's art differs from life itself to the same extent and in the same sort of way that the model of virginity which the adoring Quentin would have his sister adopt stands apart from Caddy's omnivorous sexuality. Faulkner's "mythic" portrayals of Caddy and Sutpen are false in much the same sense that the social roles he criticizes are false.

This tension between the mythic and the ironic is one of which Faulkner was acutely aware. Indeed, the open-endedness of the novels which we have examined represents his implicit acknowledgement of the gap between his indictment of Southern culture and any new framework which might succeed in reconciling the ideal and the actual. For at this stage in his artistic development, not having truly succeeded in replacing the flawed cultural *schemata* which he describes, he has attempted simultaneously to escape them in the course of fashioning works of art. His "indictment" has not yet passed over into reconstruction. But artistic success is scant consolation in the face of pervasive cultural failure, and the need for a new cultural synthesis is as urgently felt by Faulkner himself as it is by Quentin Compson, his fictional counterpart.

In *Light in August* the inherent tension between mythic and ironic modes of cultural assessment finds expression in the bifurcation of the narrative itself. The ensuing discontinuities very nearly render even aesthetic and formal completeness impossible. As Faulkner explores in explicit terms the religious self-understanding of the South, the divergence between mythic and ironic modes becomes all but unbearable, for it is as he approaches the void which lies at the very heart of his society that the bankruptcy of Southern culture is most fully—and terrifyingly—disclosed. Neither denunciation nor aesthetic retreat proves sufficient compensation for the resulting emptiness.

Faulkner's inability to formulate a new cultural synthesis to replace schemes of explanation which have ceased to explain finally reveals that the tradition of which he is unwilling heir has lost its religious center. The flawed myths which he attacks are faulty not only because they misconstrue the central facts of human existence, but, more profoundly, because they misconstrue ultimate reality itself.

In *The Sound and the Fury* Caddy is the victim of a role which perverts her sexuality in seeking to deny its very existence; but the deeper reason for her downfall is that the society which has chosen to interpret its women in these terms is guilty of idolatry. Dilsey alone manages to transcend the Compsons' tragedy, and it is precisely her Christian faith which enables her to do so. Quentin, unlike Dilsey, lacks a religious point of reference from which either to judge or to forgive his sister. In *Absalom, Absalom!*, too, it is only from the standpoint of the "Coldfield morality"—which of course includes such a point of reference—that Henry is able to renounce his part in Sutpen's plan. But the fact that Henry's ethic, like Quentin's, leads finally to his death, suggests that such a moral vision is incapable of providing any workable basis for Southern culture. Henry's Puritanism can destroy Sutpen's plan, but it cannot replace it or mold society anew. The Puritan God of Henry and Quentin is little more than an instrument of Faulkner's irony, potent for destruction but not for creation, and utterly incapable of generating a new, redemptive myth, or of providing any sort of divine charter for human society. In *Light in August* Faulkner explores this failure in powerful detail.

II

At first glance it may seem incongruous that Faulkner's most extended treatment of Southern religion should center upon characters who live almost exclusively on the periphery of their community. Lena Grove and Joe Christmas are strangers who in different ways come to obtrude on the consciousness of the Jefferson townspeople, temporarily disturbing its harmony. But even those residents of the town who become entangled with the strangers are outsiders in some sense. Byron Bunch engages in none of the pursuits which occupy his fellow mill workers in their leisure hours; his friend Gail Hightower is a disgraced minister whom the town has been unable to drive away; Joanna Burden is the descendant of a Northern abolitionist whom the town has never accepted, and Christmas's partner Brown is yet another stranger whose sojourn in Jefferson is brief. But Faulkner's concentration upon *isolés* paradoxically serves to emphasize the binding force of the community's norms, and it is on these that the novel focuses. Which is to say that Jefferson itself is the silent center of the novel.

The narrative *motif* which serves as the organizing principle of *Light in August* is the counterpoise between two very different journeys: Lena's linear migration from Alabama through Jefferson and on to Tennessee, and Joe's circular trek from Jefferson to Mottstown and back again to Jefferson and the house of Gail Hightower. In the opening scene of the novel we see Lena approaching Jefferson from the south; in the epilogue she is pushing northward through Tennessee. Joe makes his appearance in the second chapter when Byron remembers his arrival at the saw mill; in chapter nineteen Joe is killed in Jefferson after his capture in Mottstown. And, as Jefferson represents the focus of the very different journeys of Lena and Joe, so the reaction of Jefferson to these journeys reveals the moral tenor of the community.

Jefferson's treatment of Lena indicates how little value it places on the simplicity of her acceptance of the natural cycle of life, just as its complicity in the brutal death of Joe reveals the excesses to which its rigid enforcement of an arbitrary code can lead. The town's reaction to both strangers, however, discloses the same fundamental flaw in the moral standard to which it adheres. This typical Southern community is unable to reconcile the norms by which it defines itself with the reality of the human situation. Joe Christmas is the victim of a racism which denies his full humanity, and which nullifies the possibility of any compassion in those who torment and finally destroy him. In her own rejection of accepted norms Lena Grove, by contrast, reveals the extent to which Southern culture is out of rhythm with the cycles of nature that she represents.

In two senses, then, the failure of Southern culture is in the end a failure of love—a failure which stifles the expression of either *agape* or *eros*. The inability of Gail Hightower and the other Puritans whose lives become entangled with those of Lena and Joe to accommodate these outcasts within their theological system of values demonstrates that this failure is at root a religious one. While themselves peripheral members of the community, Hightower and his fellow Puritans serve nonetheless to represent those who have taken the religious formulations of their society most seriously, and so, like the two principal characters themselves, they illustrate by exaggeration the essence of the culture to which they belong.

The social norms which Lena blithely ignores and which provide the context of Joe's tragedy are in large part the creation of what Faulkner designates as "Puritanism."[7] From Hightower (who blends his Presbyterian seminary belief in Election with a constant effort to live in his grandfather's glorious past) to Doc Hines (who preaches that Negroes are predestined to hell) the Puritans of *Light in August* tend to weld the mores of their culture to a Calvinistic theology and in so doing to produce an absolutely iron-clad system. At every turn in their respective paths, Lena and Joe encounter representatives of a theological tradition which is but a handmaiden to the society with which they must deal. Indeed, the central drama of the novel arises out of the struggle between the community and the misfits who threaten it from one or another side.

III

The dominance of Puritanism in Southern culture is the thematic constant which runs through the very different stories of Lena and Joe.[8] Hightower, the only character present at the climactic episode in the story of each (the birth of Lena's baby, the death of Joe) is one in whom—though he, too, is a "Puritan"—the Southern Puritan and the Cavalier stand uneasily united. On the one hand he has been obsessed since childhood with the career of his dashing grandfather who was killed in a foolish cavalry escapade during the Civil War. On the other hand, in his professional course he has followed his father, who defied Hightower's grandfather in order to become a Presbyterian minister.

Hightower secures the pulpit of the Presbyterian church in Jefferson and proceeds to preach sermons in which the exploits of his grandfather are woven

---

[7] On Faulkner's idiosyncratic use of the term "Puritanism" see J. Robert Barth, S.J. "Faulkner and the Calvinist Tradition," in *Religious Perspectives in Faulkner's Fiction* and Brooks's treatment of the subject in *The Yoknapatawpha Country*.

[8] C. Hugh Holman has noted the important qualification that Faulkner has changed the predominantly Baptist and Methodist complexion of Yoknapatawpha to make it Presbyterian in *Light in August* ("The Unity of Faulkner's *Light in August*," *PMLA*, 73 [1958]). Faulkner has made this change in order to highlight the Calvistic bent of all the Southern Protestant churches.

into the very texture of Scripture. By preaching such sermons, Hightower attempts to project himself into the past, and seeks in this way to recapture his grandfather's evanescent moment of glory. He is in effect using his father's means in order to serve his grandfather's ends.

Though Faulkner never explicitly tells us how Hightower came by the notion that he could in effect relive his grandfather's romantic life through preaching, it is clear that elements in his father's theology which might encourage such a conception. In the drama of salvation as Calvin described it the Elect are caught up first in the destiny of Adam, who alienated man from God, and then in the life of Christ, who reconciled man to God. In this sense the human present is a recapitulation of the past; the individual reenacts the typological patterns which primordially shape the human enterprise. Christian preaching continually recreates this drama in the presentation of the Word, which is the chief vehicle of God's grace.

Hightower is, of course, intent on bringing this entire theological framework into the service of his own psychological needs. He imagines that his life has been predestined, and, by preaching about his romantic forebear, he hopes to incorporate himself into the archetype which he believes his grandfather to represent. His sermons signify his attempt to annul the threatening present by means of a narrative which seeks to repeat the "divine" moment from his grandfather's past. Byron Bunch later hears Hightower's ministry characterized in the following terms: "The dogma he was supposed to preach [was] all full of galloping cavalry and defeat and glory just as when he tried to tell them on the street about the galloping horses, it in turn would get all mixed up with absolution and choirs of martial seraphim, until it was natural that the old men and women should believe that what he preached in God's own house on God's own day verged on actual sacrilege'' (57).[9] Hightower's parishioners and, indeed, most of Faulkner's readers are puzzled by the way in which Hightower conflates dogma and derring-do, but in fact the connections between them are of crucial importance for the novel as a whole, and they extend far beyond the peculiar psychological transferences we have discussed.

It would appear that Hightower's Puritan father, and his Cavalier grandfather were men almost identical in attitude and cast of mind. Both were men who practiced "simple adherence to a simple code" (446). They were rugged individualists who made their way in the world through "main strength and . . . the devil's grace. . . . " Both were "throwbacks to the austere and not dim times not so long passed, when a man in that country had little of himself to waste and little time to do it in, and had to guard and protect that little not

---

[9]*Light in August* (New York: Random House, 1968; Modern Library College Edition, first edition). All succeeding page numbers refer to this edition.

only from nature but from man too, by means of a sheer fortitude that did not offer, in this lifetime anyway, physical ease or reward'' (448). Whether the goal at issue was the establishment of the baronial splendor of a landed gentleman or the convening of God's elect in a virgin promised land, the means by which success could be attained was fortitude of will, absolute commitment to the dictates of one's "simple code."

Puritan and Cavalier alike see both the land and the time in which they are placed as blanks on which to carve their names. Though they conceive the outcome of their efforts to be determined by Providence or Fate, they see themselves, nevertheless as the captains of their own destiny. The fatalism of the Calvinist who looks at the war-ravaged fields and says, "God will provide," is matched by the fatalism of his Cavalier father who rode nonchalantly through enemy lines believing that only the bullet which Chance had set aside for him would claim its mark. But equal in power to this fatalism in its influence on the mind of Puritan and Cavalier is the accompanying belief in the potency of the disciplined human will. In the case of the Hightowers, father and son are secretly proud of each other in spite of their differences, for each has carried out his intentions in the face of nearly overwhelming difficulties. Each comes even to admire the recalcitrance of the other.

A third feature common to Puritan and Cavalier as Faulkner describes them is an indifference to the external world. The obverse of the belief that nature is a *tabula rasa* awaiting man's shaping hand is the assumption that nature lacks an inherent integrity or worth. And such an orientation necessarily has a corrosive effect upon human relations. For if what matters most is the successful implementation of one's stated intentions, then the wishes and feelings of others are of comparatively little moment. Other people are part of the external world which one must shape in one's own image, not centers of autonomous personhood with any value in their own right.

Such an individualism is exemplified in the attitude of Hightower's father toward both his wife and the war. Grandfather Hightower shrewdly observes that it did not matter whom his minister son finally settled upon as a mate, so long as she could sing alto from a Presbyterian hymn book. And the son commits himself only to those whom he believes able to assist him in forwarding his design. Though an abolitionist by conviction, he enlists as a chaplain in the Confederate army. So long as he is free to maintain his convictions and to preach them, he sees no contradiction in supporting troops which are fighting for principles antithetical to his own. He is thus, as Faulkner notes, "two separate and complete people, one of whom dwelled by serene rules in a world where reality did not exist" (448).

A like pattern seems to have governed the behavior of Hightower's Cavalier grandfather, so far as we can tell on the basis of the stories which the boy hears of him. In any case the absurd but heroic deed for which his namesake idolizes him was an act of conspicuous and pointless willfulness. Gail Hightower the cavalryman was killed while robbing a henhouse in a town occupied by enemy troops. Tired of living on the poor fare available to a nearly destitute army, he simply ignored the presence of the Federal force and rode into a barnyard where he was shot—not, as we might expect by a Yankee sharpshooter but instead by an enraged housewife. In this reckless act, which bears no relation to the cause for which he was purportedly fighting, Hightower's grandfather demonstrates an indifference to the plain facts of his situation which equals, in its own way, the obtuseness of his son who also insists on living by "serene rules in a world where reality does not exist." So the seemingly incongruous mixture of Calvinistic theology and martial romanticism which characterizes Gail Hightower's sermons is not as inexplicable as at first it appears, for he is "propped upright, as it were, between puritan and cavalier."

But Hightower goes his forebears one better. While they were each "two separate and complete people" contained in the same body, one practical, the other idealistic, Gail himself is only one, for he has no "practical" side. In fact he lives in a reverie which seeks to annul the present altogether and to take him back to that central moment "thirty years before he was born." But in the life which he chooses to ignore—that is, his daily life in the here and now—he reenacts the pattern of his forebears in ways which he does not recognize.

Like his father before him, Hightower marries a woman who is attractive to him chiefly because she is useful in furthering his design. Thereafter he ignores her, even when she takes lovers in Memphis in a desperate search for some mutuality of affection. He is fully as much a phantom to her as ever his father was to him in the household where Hightower grew up. And when the younger Hightower's wife finally kills herself by jumping from a Memphis hotel window, a photographer catches him with a look of "satanic glee" on his face, proud despite himself of the single-mindedness with which he has maintained his pulpit in total disregard of the seamy scandal which now engulfs him.

Hightower's relation to the Jefferson community in a certain sense reenacts his father's paradoxical relationship to the Southern cause during the Civil War. Completely oblivious of the real needs and expectations of his parish before the scandal, Hightower nonetheless resists his fellow townsmen's every effort to drive him from their midst after he loses his post. Despite the beatings he receives, he maintains that his tormenters are "good people" and stubbornly remains in Jefferson. Like his father before him, Hightower proves unable to renounce the society from which his own dream has expelled him. The abolitionist father finally joins the Confederate army; the son refuses to leave his flock even when it rejects him. Such tenacity represents an unconscious acknowledgment that some sort of community, however deeply flawed, is necessary for human life. As Faulkner views the matter, the Hightowers' paradoxical commitment to Southern society is, in the end, a tacit admission that the world in which their ideals exist is imaginary, and that the "immoral" but real community is a necessary counterbalance to such fantasies.

From the perspective of Jefferson itself, of course, matters take on a different complexion. For good or for ill, Hightower provides the town with a moral point of reference which it would otherwise lack, and over the course of his career he fulfills this function in a number of ways. At the beginning of his ministry the residents of Jefferson expect Hightower as a man of God to provide a model for upright conduct. The minister is necessary as a living example of the behavior the town expects of itself, whether or not it follows his lead. Once the scandal involving Hightower's wife is felt to disqualify the preacher for such a role, however, the town turns on him in the name of the morality which in their eyes he has flouted, and he suddenly becomes not shepherd but scapegoat. At last this stage, too, passes, and Hightower, though remaining on the periphery of the local scene, wins a kind of acceptance. Having weathered a storm of hatred, he is granted a measure of tolerance and even of occasional support by alms, for the community obscurely feels him, despite his eccentricity, to represent a moral standard of which it needs to have in its midst a living embodiment.[10]

With the notable exception of its racism, Hightower endorses the code of behavior by which Jefferson orders its life. Byron Bunch, an indefatigable worker who leaves the sawmill only to sleep and keep the Sabbath, looks to Hightower as his spiritual mentor, for to him the defrocked clergyman remains a representative of the religious ideal to which, presumably, the town gives its suffrage. Indeed, when Byron asks Hightower to come to the aid of Lena and Joe, he rightly believes that he is appealing to the wisest religious figure in Jefferson.

IV

The Puritanism which forms the milieu of the novel is further defined by the McEacherns, who, with Hightower stand closest to the religious center of Yoknapatawpha society, for they are the very type of the Southern Calvinists

---

[10]The contrast I am here drawing is given a more general treatment by Panthea Reid Broughton in her work, *William Faulkner: The Abstract and the Actual* (Baton Rouge LA: LSU Press, 1974). I am in her debt for calling attention to this aspect of Faulkner's fiction, but I cannot accept her interpretation of it. In Broughton's reading, Faulkner not only acknowledges the disjointedness of "the abstract and the actual" in modern life, but effectively reunites them through his art. I am arguing that Faulkner's best fiction is haunted by the conviction that human consciousness is irremediably alienated from nature, and that therefore no bridge can be built between life and the verities.

who serve as the moral watchdogs of this community, living as they do in accordance with the Protestant work ethic beneath the watchful eye of a wrathful God. The God of Simon McEachern is a keeper of strict accounts who grants salvation to the Elect, to those whom he enables to fulfill the contractual terms spelled out by Scripture and by the Westminster Confession. And it is thus no accident that McEachern's relations with his adopted son, Joe Christmas, begin with a contract negotiated with the matron of the orphanage in which Joe has been placed.

To the matron, no less than to McEachern, the adoption proceedings are "a matter for the two parties to settle between themselves" (134). McEachern makes the terms of the agreement clear: Joe "will find food and shelter and the care of Christian people." In return he must learn "that the two abominations are sloth and idle thinking, the two virtues are work and the fear of God" (135). Joe himself believes that his assignment to McEachern is the price to be paid for the "promissory note" he signed by stealing a tube of toothpaste, and thus, he, too feels that the new relation is contractual.

The drama of Joe's life with the McEacherns is to be—in the mind of his adoptive father at least—a reenactment of the process of salvation. From McEachern's point of view, Joe, despite his dubious origins and the bleak future which they would seem to foretell, has been rescued by a benevolent adoptive father who requires only that he abide by the father's moral code. The analogies between this arrangement and the doctrines of original sin, redemption, and sanctification as McEachern would have understood them are clear. For McEachern as for the Hightowers, human agency is little more than a matter of accepting or rejecting preordained patterns of living. McEachern "saves" Joe from what he takes to be the high road to damnation and places him on the narrow path of the God-fearing, hard-working saint.

McEachern exemplifies the Puritan combination of extreme emphasis on the individual will and a profound theological fatalism. He is sure of the necessity of the back-breaking regimen he imposes on himself and his family, and equally sure that the result of that labor will come, not of his own effort, but as God wills. Thus, when the enraged adoptive father pursues his wayward son to the dancehall, he is as certain of his duty as he is indifferent to its consequences. McEachern is a man, in short, for whom the word surprise can have no meaning, because human action and divine response are not, from his perspective, causally related. He expects nothing, no concrete result whatsoever; the human person can do or fail to do his duty, but in either case his efforts have no effect on events in the world, since history is entirely in God's hands.

McEachern's fatalism and sense of duty are reflected in his attitude toward nature. For him, nature is simply the stage on which the drama of the divine-human encounter is acted out. His land and his livestock are objects for which he is accountable, but they have no intrinsic worth. His cows represent to him so many dollars or gallons of milk, his crops he sees as mere commodities. When Joe sells the heifer his father has given him, McEachern is angered not by the loss of the animal but by the bad bargain Joe has driven and the sinful use to which he intends to put the money. Nature lives only as a thing to be managed, as a store of potential possessions which are perhaps a sign of divine favor but which have no life or worth of their own.

McEachern's view of women is of a piece with his attitude toward all other terrestrial things. His wife is simply a necessary element in the earthly enterprise of the God-fearing Presbyterian man. He sees her, no less than Joe, as a kind of child subject to his discipline. Such a conception makes no provision for sexual passion within a marriage, and we may surmise that McEachern sees conjugal sex as another form of the "lechery" of which he accuses Joe. Mrs. McEachern, like Hightower's wife, is a frustrated and emotionally starved woman. She bears, Faulkner tells us, no distinguishing sexual features whatsoever, except a dress and a knot of hair. Her clumsy affection for Joe serves as the only outlet for her femininity. Except for his inability to make her produce a child, McEachern has been as successful in subduing his wife to the demands of his creed as he has been in imposing order on his pastures and fields. To acknowledge the otherness of his wife or to allow himself to feel sexual passion would be to displace the sovereign will by which he shapes his world to conform to God's ordinances.

For McEachern the duty of the saint is to repeat in a limited way the actions of God himself by imposing rational order on the world which he has been given. To concede to nature any life or integrity of its own is to make of it a temptation which would threaten the entire Puritan project. Thus McEachern, as Faulkner repeatedly reminds us, is a man "ruthless and just, but not unkind." Like Hightower, he is simply determined to make the human heart, and indeed the whole of nature, fit the Procrustean bed of his preconceptions.

But while McEachern shares with Hightower a commitment to this general Puritan worldview, both in his relation to the community and in the nature of his fantasy, he also differs in certain respects from the failed preacher. McEachern lacks Hightower's intellectual disposition and Cavalier heritage; his mind thus retains a decidedly this-worldly cast which Hightower has lost. McEachern shows none of Hightower's obsession with the Southern past, and certainly he is not tempted to recapture its futile glory through fantasy. Nevertheless, he no less than Hightower lives according to "serene rules where reality does not exist," and thus he acts out a sort of fantasy albeit one which is untouched by nostalgic reverie.

The fantastic quality of McEachern's Puritanism becomes apparent in his reaction to Joe's rebellious "whoring." McEachern learns that Joe has been engaged in a surreptitious affair with a local prostitute. He comes to this discovery not so much by observing the plain evidence of hidden suit and missing cow as by the clairvoyant power of his brooding over "lechery" and over the mechanics of an evil about which he has no first-hand knowledge. In fact, so detached is his mind from the actual events transpiring before him that he does not even see Joe climb down a rope that dangles outside the bedroom window where McEachern lies deep in open-eyed thought (189).

When McEachern finally realizes that Joe is escaping to his lover, he responds with "pure and impersonal outrage," as if it were not he who had been insulted but a divinely instituted court—a court of which he is the judge. Without taking note even of the direction of the car in which Joe is riding, McEachern pursues him on a draft horse as if "known destination and speed were not necessary" (190). And when he arrives at the school house in which Joe and Bobbie are dancing, he believes that he has been divinely guided and "propelled by some militant Michael Himself." Though to others his actions seem outrageous and frenzied as he runs into the room and denounces Bobbie as a Jezebel, to himself he seems "to be standing just and rocklike and with neither haste nor anger while on all sides the sluttishness of weak human men seeth[es] in a long sigh of terror about the actual representative of the wrathful and retributive Throne." When the enraged Joe swings a chair at his head, McEachern greets the attack "in the furious and dreamlike exaltation of a martyr who has already been absolved." He falls "astonished a little, but not much, and not for long" (191–92).

In this episode McEachern's understanding of his actions is as fantastic as Hightower's sermons. So completely is his consciousness dominated by a wrathful, Calvinistic God eager to punish the transgressors of His moral code, that McEachern sees no distinction whatever between his vision and the reality it seeks to explain; neither can he distinguish himself from the role he believes himself to be playing in the drama he has imagined. Like his unsuccessful efforts at instilling the virtues of love for work and fear of God, his last attempt to punish Joe fails because the form into which he forces experience cannot contain it. When McEachern bursts into the school house, we see not the archangel Michael but a crazed old man who is determined to force his will on a young man who is now fully his equal in will and strength. Just as Hightower preaches to an empty church, McEachern flails away at a devil who is not there, and falls victim to the murderous chair which his fantasy would not allow him to see. So far has McEachern's obsession separated him from reality that, when the blow falls, he is barely surprised; not even the threat of death can shake his illusions. McEachern's failure to comprehend the full complexity of life is even more dramatic than Hightower's. Like Hightower, his attempts at ethical action are thwarted by his blind investment in an abstract scheme which simply denies what it cannot explain.

McEachern's relationship to his community is similar to Hightower's in that he, too, stands at the periphery of its life by virtue of taking its stated moral and theological assumptions with absolute seriousness. In McEachern's view the town is full of snares and delusions, but only because it does not enforce its own ethical standards. He warns Joe that only a man who has learned the ways of the world and reached moral maturity can safely navigate his way among its pitfalls. He is especially wary of the cafe owned by the Memphis bootlegger and of the transient railroad men to whom it caters. But, of course, in his disapproval of this group we can assume that McEachern is voicing the consensus of town opinion. No doubt the sober churchgoing townspeople of this unnamed village would also object to the dance which McEachern disrupts. The mark which distinguishes McEachern from the majority of the townsfolk is the violence of his convictions. As is also true of Hightower, McEachern's differences with the town on ethical issues are largely matters of degree: McEachern holds himself aloof in order to avoid the compromises with evil which most townspeople must make for economic reasons, but within the relative isolation of his farm he is simply protecting the purity of the moral code by which the town itself lives—or which in any case, it espouses.

McEachern's relationship to his community differs from Hightower's, however, in that McEachern is able to sustain his distance. Hightower, both by virtue of his profession and because first his wife and then Byron Bunch intrude on his reveries, is pulled against his will into the mainstream of Jefferson life. McEachern's fantasy, by contrast, is exposed only at his death, and he therefore never publicly has to live out the consequences of his failure. But when at last McEachern falls under the blow of his enraged stepson, he leaves behind an unintended audience that is as uncomprehending of the Biblical judgments and apocalyptic vision which once comprised his private reality as Jefferson once was puzzled by Hightower's mad sermons. In both cases, the religious vision which performs a unifying function in the community has within the context of a particular mind intensified into a fanaticism which the town cannot accept.

In Hightower Faulkner has thus extended and explored the kind of religious character which McEachern represents. McEachern is a man of the same class and sensibility as most of Hightower's parishioners; yet his Calvinistic rigidity drives him into the same sort of madness which infects the intellectual preacher. While the content of Hightower's fantasy differs significantly from McEachern's, its form is essentially the same. Each man believes himself to be an actor in a preordained divine plan in which he either directly or vicariously plays a glorious role. The successful implementation of this plan requires at once an absolute concentration of the will and an absolute confidence in the power of God to complete his purposes. Both Puritans, in short, are at the same time willful and fatalistic. The fact that the two men share a common psychology suggests that each has simply taken the theological understanding of his community to its logical conclusion, which is paradoxically anti-communal. McEachern stands between Hightower and his church members on the scale of reality-defying abstraction and self-absorption, but they all stand together on the same continuum, and its name is Puritanism.

V

The last of Faulkner's major Puritan figures in *Light in August* is one who is never accepted by her community. Joanna Burden is the product of a New England family that was led by abolitionist sentiments to settle in Jefferson after the Civil War. When we meet her in the novel, Joanna has lived her entire life in isolation both from the white community which considers her a traitorous "nigger-lover" and from the black population for whom she is a mysterious benefactress.

In many ways Miss Burden is less at home in Yoknapatawpha than any of its other inhabitants. Not only is she a Northerner by heritage and training but her very presence in Jefferson is meant as a challenge to the racial mores which are the most distinctive feature of Southern life. It is therefore all the more startling to discover that the religious vision which shapes her life is another aspect of the same Puritanism that shapes Southern culture. Faulkner has in this character once again given us a figure who stands at the periphery of the community, excluded because of having taken its own religious presuppositions with utmost seriousness. As we shall see, Joanna Burden's disagreement with the citizens of Jefferson on questions of race is not nearly as important as the Puritanism they share, and it is her religion which makes her in the end an exemplar of the same kind of inhumanity represented by the townspeople, though in them it expresses itself in a racism which she opposes.

Indeed, her father and grandfather appear to have borne a remarkable resemblance to Hightower's forebears. If between them Hightower's father and grandfather divided the roles of puritan and cavalier, Joanna's immediate male ancestors each combined the two. The Burdens were adventurers, capable of making a fortune with gun and shovel and ready to kill those who defended slavery. The elder Calvin Burden indoctrinated his son as determinedly as ever Simon McEachern catechizes Joe, although Joanna's grandfather was likely to be drunk when conducting the lesson. The mail-order message that Joanna's father uses to procure her mother as a bride reminds us of Hightower's grandfather's observation that his son would have married any woman who could sing alto. And, like Hightower's grandfather, Joanna's grandfather and half-brother are gunned down in the streets of Jefferson.

The similarities in external shape between the lives of the male Burdens and the other Puritans we have discussed is matched by what we know of their respective theological visions. The elder Calvin imbues in his son two hatreds that match the two virtues which McEachern attempts to teach Joe. " 'I'll learn you to hate two things,' " he says, " 'hell and slaveholders' " (229). The rest of the world can go to its own "benighted hell," but Burden is determined to "beat the loving God into [my children] as long as I can raise my arm" (230). This determination to see the ways of the "loving God" enforced, even if by the harshest means, is typical of Faulkner's Puritans. In the case of Calvin Burden, Sr., it is manifested not only in child-rearing (as with McEachern) but also in the zeal with which he, like Hightower's father, seeks to transform the Mississippi wilderness into his own version of the Promised Land.

Burden's abolitionist doctrine is as fanatical as Hightower's sermons or McEachern's visions. In the middle of his son's wedding he breaks into a speech in which we are told that he "dared any man there to deny that Lincoln and the negro and Moses and the children of Israel were the same, and that the Red Sea was just the blood that had to be spilled in order that the black race might cross over into the Promised Land" (238). Like his Puritan brothers, Burden is more or less oblivious to the moment in which he lives, and to the actual people of whom he here speaks. America is to him a stage on which a divine play is being enacted, and he is determined to play the part of one of the righteous. It is in this spirit that he comes to Jefferson, a town which he has never seen, in order to remove from it the curse of slavery.

This sounds promising enough, but in fact Burden is not sympathetic to blacks; his motives are of a different kind, for he believes that slavery has put a curse on black and white alike. He takes up his work in Jefferson not out of any love for white or black, but in order to remove the theological guilt in which slavery has steeped the land. He sees himself and those who join him in the cause of liberation as agents in a massive rite of purification. The black man is a burden of which the white man seeks to be free.

> "Damn, lowbuilt black folks: lowbuilt because of the weight of the wrath of God, black because of the sin of human bondage staining their blood and flesh." His gaze was vague, fanatical, and convinced. "But we done freed them now, both black and white alike. They'll bleach out now. In a hundred years they will be white folks again. Then maybe we'll let them come back into America" (234).

Here blackness itself is seen as a sign of bondage and a curse. Burden's aim is not to recognize the humanity of the black but to transform him into a white. The purpose of Burden's crusade to expiate the sin of blackness is to preserve the purity of America, which we can assume has for him a divinely privileged status.

Calvin's son Nathaniel passes on the same understanding of the curse of blackness to his daughter Joanna when he shows her the graves of her murdered brother and grandfather.

> "Remember this. Your grandfather and brother are lying there, murdered not by one white man but by the curse which God put on a whole race before your grandfather or your brother or me or you were even thought of. A race doomed and cursed forever and ever a part of the white race's doom and curse for its sins. . . . The curse of every white child that ever was born and that ever will be born. None can escape it" (239).

The distinctly personal tone of this last of the Burden pronouncements on the race question makes explicit the connection between the Negro and the Puritan's own destiny. The Burdens, though in one sense outsiders so far as the "Southern problem" is concerned, are in their own minds at least unavoidably affected by it. The curse of slavery here takes on the overtones of original sin; every human being is infected with its pollution by virtue of his membership in the human community. As abolitionists, therefore, the Burdens are working not so much for the liberation of the Negro as for their own salvation. Calvin Burden and his descendants, no less than Hightower or McEachern, are driven by their own demons to enforce a private theological vision on the world in order to claim their place in what they conceive to be a divine plan of salvation.

Calvin Burden descries the black curse at work in his own family. On seeing his dark grandson he exclaims, "Folks will think I bred to a damn slaver" (234). He identifies the dark side of his own family with the Negroes he hopes to free. It is no wonder, then, that his granddaughter has childhood visions of white babies enveloped in black shadows "as if they were nailed to the cross" (239).

The Burdens, no less than the unambiguously Southern Puritans whom Faulkner scrutinizes, are single-minded in their fanatical understanding of God's purposes; they lack any qualifying sense of the integrity of society or of nature. Once again, human life is entirely a matter of the individual will's aligning or refusing to align itself with the manifest will of God. The sign of one's divine election is membership in a society which conducts itself according to God's law and whose history visibly enacts the divine plan. The Burdens, like the other Puritans in *Light in August,* therefore seek to impose their radical vision upon the community in which they find themselves.

Similarly, the view of blacks which Calvin Burden and his son express is not in the end so very different from that of the white natives of Yoknapatawpha. In the words of Faulkner critic Thadious Davis, blacks "remain inferior to whites, yet they are the means by which whites may work out their own expiation."[11] The Burdens have simply made the black curse the object of

---

[11]*Faulkner's "Negro"* (Baton Rouge: LSU Press, 1983), 144.

their Calvinistic zeal, and it is the obsessiveness of their concern as much as any other factor which has alienated them from the community with which at a deeper level they stand in sympathy. In this way, too, they resemble Hightower and McEachern, for they have taken a limited facet of the accepted religious framework of the culture with such passionate seriousness that the result is an obsession which the community can no longer understand.

The degree to which the Burdens fit the pattern of Southern religiosity is illustrated by their spiritual kinship to Doc Hines, Joe Christmas's fanatical grandfather. Hines sees himself as God's "chosen instrument" (365) who presides over the inevitable drama of judgment and destruction set in motion by his daughter's "bitchery and abomination" (353) when she slept with a circus man who may have been a Negro, and conceived Joe as a result. Most of Hines's adult life is taken up in the coils of an apocalyptic fantasy of the sort McEachern embraces only at the conclusion of his story. He hovers like an avenging angel (or demon) over the orphanage which is Joe's first home, and returns at the climax of Joe's tragedy to urge the outraged white population to kill his grandson.

Between times, Hines occupies himself with seizing the pulpits of black churches "to preach to them humility before all skins lighter than theirs, preaching the superiority of the white race, himself his own exhibit A, in fanatic and unconscious paradox" (325). In this passage we see what amounts to a conflation of the image of Hightower with the doctrine of Calvin Burden. Hines is a man trapped in his own fanatical vision who is driven to bend his social world into the shape of his obsession; in the process, he renders himself unintelligible to those around him. The anti-gospel he preaches to the Negroes is a Southern version of the notion of the "black curse" which in the Burden family excites the abolitionist reformer's zeal. Though Hines is protected as a merely eccentric member of the white community (he, after all, toes the line on the race question), there is, in a certain sense, little difference between him and the hated Burdens. The people of Mottstown know Hines to be what McEachern and the Burdens actually are: zealots who have taken the religious tenets of the community to the last extreme.

In the Puritan framework of the novel, the Negro race itself is cursed and must be removed if the community is to become pure and righteous. The presence of the Negro is a sign of divine disfavor which proves that the South is not, while under the curse, a part of God's elected community. Whether the Puritan's attitude toward the Negro is one of guilt, as in the case of the Burdens, or of unmixed hatred, as in the case of Hines, he believes that the black curse will last until the white race is free of Negro contamination. The Burdens seek to accomplish this end by paying off the moral debt which binds the white man to the Negro, Hines by insisting that blacks are of a different species from whites and seeking to erect an absolute barrier between the two.

Miscegenation, by either measure, becomes the ultimate abomination, and the lust incited by women is its cause.

For the Puritan, women and Negroes alike represent a potential source of contamination. Women are objects of lust who in their natural state are themselves lustful, and who may thus ensnare the unwary man in the coils of fleshly pleasure which is in itself a signal evil. But women are an even greater curse as a temptation to miscegenation. Sexual passion, an evil in itself because it threatens the will's rational pursuit of God's plan, is doubly dangerous when it jeopardizes racial purity. To the imagination of the Southern Puritan Negroes and women are both creatures of the corrupted natural order which is the arena of unbridled desire.

The choice accordingly faced by a Puritan woman such as Joanna Burden is between becoming the dark seductress which men believe women in their natural state to be, and developing in herself the coldly rational will of the Puritan man. Joanna chooses both by turns. Early in their relationship Joe Christmas notices in Joanna a "dual personality." On the one hand she is a woman in whom he sees "a horizon of physical security and adultery if not pleasure;" on the other he sees "the mantrained muscles and the mantrained habit of thinking born of heritage and environment" against which he must struggle (221–22). As their affair progresses she alternatively conforms to each of these models.

At first Joanna gives in to Joe's sexual advances as if she were a man struggling with another man "for an object of no actual value to either, for which they struggled on principle alone" (222): she initially brings to her new role of sex partner the same hard masculinity she uses to manage the financial affairs of the Negro schools which she capably serves as trustee. Then suddenly she plunges into a period of wild lust which makes Joe feel as though "he had fallen into a sewer" (242). During this phase Joanna remains by day a sober benefactress, but at night she becomes a dark temptress who hides hot and half-naked, waiting for Joe to discover and ravage her. In the final stage of the affair Joanna attempts not only to repent of the actions which she believes have damned her "forever to the hell of her forefathers" (244) but to redeem Joe by forcing him to become a respectable Negro lawyer. At this point she reverts to her original mannish persona and tries to reform Joe in much the way that McEachern had done before her. The prayer in which she recounts her own sin and seeks to bring Joe to repentance is almost a repetition of the earlier scene in which McEachern asks God's forgiveness for chastising Joe even as he makes a final effort at forcing Joe to learn his catechism.

Joanna's sexual history shows that she is incapable of what Faulkner calls "a life of healthy and normal sin" (246). The poles of depravity and morbid remorse between which she vacillates allow no sane middle ground in which a wholesome sexuality might take root. Joanna finally accepts the narrow view of her Puritan forefathers, that femininity means either lust or a limp asexual passivity, and in the end she chooses to forsake the role of woman altogether. In her relationship with Joe she abandons the role of lover to take up that of preacher, and so seeks to subdue Joe to her will, which she identifies with the will of God.

The sterility of this relationship is symbolized by the supposed pregnancy which proves to be menopause. Like the life-denying fanaticism which leads Joanna to reject her femininity altogether, her affair with Joe signals not the beginning of new life but the end of her family's line. Joanna's inability to bring her emotions and sexuality into harmony with her theological vision leaves her no point of contact with Joe other than that provided by a raw struggle of wills. Joe and Joanna are both martyrs to the Puritan scheme of salvation: Joannna's obsessive commitment to it and Joe's rebellious rejection of it together constitute the only field on which they can meet, and the fruit of their encounter is mutual destruction. The ascetic devotion to a view of God which recognizes the attribute of will and little more leads to a conception of humanity which denies the claims of any faculty besides the will. Under such conditions human relations can be only struggles for dominance, whether or not they are recognized as such.

Joe and Joanna are finally little more to each other than objects of manipulation. Joanna first loses her independence to Joe, then seeks to make him the instrument of her damnation, and finally turns upon him by demanding that he surrender himself to the will of God as she has done. Joe conquers her body, and Joanna retaliates by making him the pawn of her Puritan God. Both as instrument of her damnation and as object of her reformer's zeal Joe is simply acting out the play which Joanna imagines that God has written. And Joe is perfect for the part because he believes himself to be a Negro. He is thus the symbol of that burden with which Joanna believes she is cursed. In breaking at once the Puritan taboo against fornication and the taboo against miscegenation, she incurs the wrath of the God whom her father has taught her to believe has already condemned her. By madly attempting to rehabilitate Joe she hopes to lift the curse to which she has subjected herself, and so to complete the scheme of salvation.

Joanna Burden thus stands revealed as Faulkner's paradigmatic female Puritan. She repeats the pattern which we have seen exemplified in Faulkner's male Puritans but embodies the peculiar qualities of the Puritan woman as well. Like that of Martha Armstid and of Mrs. McEachern, Joanna's femininity has been stifled. Locked into a male-dominated world in which the triumph of the individual will is the highest value, Joanna employs her womanly resources toward the end of self-assertion. Joe is right to suspect that Joanna's favors, like the surreptitious food his stepmother prepared for him, are enticements intended to lead him into subjugation. Joe's recollection of the McEacherns as he eats the first bite of stolen food at Joanna Burden's suggests already that in this house he will encounter both the male and female forms of the Puritan will to power.

VI

When Joe Christmas encounters Joanna Burden he meets the last of a series of Puritans who have sought to shape his life. And he meets in her the female image of himself: like hers his psyche has been molded by a fascination with race and sex, and, like hers, his ideas about both have been filtered through the distorting spectacles of Puritanism. But, while Joanna's revolt against the taboos of her heritage is short-lived and incomplete, Joe's is total. Joanna is the sometime sinner who would be saved; Joe is the rebel who chooses damnation. In his solitary protest against the religious system which has formed him, however, Joe is entirely a creature of the culture which he reflects. Although he entirely lacks the self-consciousness that would allow him to articulate the criticisms of Puritanism which Faulkner expresses through him, Joe's tragedy lies at the heart of Faulkner's indictment of Southern religiosity. He is Faulkner's anti-Puritan Puritan whose death is a nonredemptive sacrifice to a higher religious vision which Faulkner himself cannot fully encompass.

From his first moment of consciousness Joe is made to look at the world through Puritan lenses. In the orphanage he learns to expect punishment for pleasure, and through the agency of Doc Hines he begins to think of himself as a "nigger," one marked by an ineradicable curse. These lessons are driven home to him in his first encounter with sexuality, when he is caught stealing toothpaste by a dietician who unexpectedly returns to her room with her lover. The terrified four-year-old who gorges himself on toothpaste while listening to a bout of illicit love-making receives in the process a memorable lesson: pleasure and evil are causally linked. It is significant for Joe's later life that the specific pleasures here condemned are those of eating and sex. The very activities which sustain and propagate life thus bear for him the label of sin. Joe is being unconsciously shaped for the moment when he must choose between a life which can be sustained only by evil, and a goodness which can be achieved only through death.

Indeed, Doc Hines preaches to Joe that this choice has already been made for him by the fact of his Negro blood. For Hines it is inevitable that Joe should be caught up in "bitchery and abomination," because his existence is the result of miscegenation. The very act which gave Joe life and the very blood which flows through his veins mark him as one of the damned. Joe absorbs from his grandfather the belief that the horrible course of his life is already set, and it is a notion from which he is never able to free himself.

At the home of McEachern such notions are reinforced. Joe learns to fear both the male who exacts punishments and the female protector who seeks to control him by favors rather than by force. The orphan who has only his belief that he is cursed to give him a sense of distinction and identity clings to his "sin" as the badge of his freedom. Joe sees the efforts of the McEacherns to reform him and make him their son as an attempt to strip him of his identity. Joe chooses the doom which his grandfather has pronounced as a way of claiming the only freedom he knows. Here, too, however, his destiny is determined; he can avoid the path of salvation only by setting out to ensure that he is damned. In his hard-headed choice of what McEachern has taught him to regard as a life of sin, Joe is simply a Puritan in reverse. He is determined to live a life which gives evidence of his election to damnation, and therefore to claim the place which a merciless God has alloted him.

The paradox of human will and divine determination which we have noted in Faulkner's Puritans finds its mirror image in Joe. The history of his interaction with his step-parents is the record of one long struggle of wills. He refuses to submit to them on principle, regardless of the cost to himself. Yet the independence he wins from them is lost to a sense of fate as rigid as McEachern's own rules. Joe's negative Puritanism is most clearly seen in his refusal to learn his catechism and in his first sexual experiences. When he flouts McEachern's command to memorize the Presbyterian catechism he does so not with maniacal glee, but with a quiet resoluteness. As he stares at the page in determined incomprehension, he wears "a rapt, calm expression like a monk in a picture" (140). This entire scene is cast in terms which suggest that Joe's rebellion against McEachern's religion is in itself a holy crusade. The faithfully performed ritual of violence during which Joe holds the book for exactly an hour in the attitude of "a Catholic choir boy" (140), then submits to McEachern's methodical beatings delivered "without heat or force," suggests Joe's confirmation in his own negative Puritanism.

In the novel the catechism scene is followed immediately by Joe's first experience of sex. Here again, somewhat paradoxically, Joe accepts as his conceptual model the Puritan schema of salvation. His friends have lured a Negro girl into a barn to gang-rape her, and when Joe's turn comes he lashes out at her, outraged at the degradation which coupling with her would mean. Similarly, his revulsion upon hearing menstruation described is relieved only by killing a sheep and drenching his hands in its blood. In both cases Joe's horror of the animality of sex is expressed in an act of violence.

The last stage in Joe's development comes during the course of his affair with the waitress-prostitute Bobbie. In this his first full-fledged sexual relationship, Joe seems to overcome his revulsion against the physical, but in fact his hidden hatred reemerges in the more potent guise of sado-masochism. Joe begins his courtship of Bobbie in the naive belief that she is as innocent as he and that they will find together the love and mutual respect which neither of them has yet known. But this romantic dream is shattered with her confession on their first date that she is menstruating and then by her renunciation of him on account of his presumed Negro blood.

Joe's experience with Bobbie destroys the only obstacle that has stood between him and the path of self-destruction which opened in his battle with McEachern. Bobbie, whom he originally saw as the pure object of an ideal love, proves to be the whore McEachern believes all women in their natural state to be. Instead of accepting him as a man despite the suspicion of "niggerness" that hangs over him, she turns his confession against him and rejects him for it. The connection between the inherent evil of sex and the curse of blackness is convincingly reasserted in Joe's mind as his last youthful attempt to elude the fate which Doc Hines has pronounced upon him is thwarted.

Fittingly, Joe's youth ends with the act of patricide. Though we are never certain that his stepfather died from the blow of the chair, Joe's murderous intent is clear. He attacks McEachern, returns to the farm, and departs with horse and money in an exact reversal of the actions which brought McEachern to the oneroom schoolhouse. When at the end of his furious ride on the much-abused farm horse Joe springs "full and of his own accord" into the fist of Bobbie's new protector, he does so "with something of the exaltation of his adopted father" (204–205). Joe has freed himself from McEachern, but not from the mindset which is his legacy. In his hatred of women and Negroes, his belief that sex and eating are inherently evil, and his conviction that his dignity depends on following the dictates of his will, Joe remains a Puritan.

When Joe murders Joanna Burden and is subsequently killed by the fanatical vigilante Percy Grimm, he simply completes the Puritan drama which began at his birth. Faulkner describes Joe's final week as a strangely circular attempt at escape which ends where it began; for Joe escape and entrapment are identical. Faulkner's anti-Puritan is imprisoned by the very structure against which he rebels; he has internalized the world-view which is in the deepest sense his true enemy. In rejecting the Calvinistic way of salvation which McEachern and Joanna have attempted to force upon him, Joe finds himself embarked on the equally narrow road to damnation. His flight from the tyranny of Puritanism turns out only to represent the downward arc of the Puritan circle.

The brokenness of Joe's life is brilliantly illustrated on the day of Joanna's murder. As he contemplates the crime which he is about to commit, he feels at once fated and willful. The murder is both something that is going to happen to him and something he is going to do (97). He rightly sees the deed as the culmination of his rebellion against the Puritan God, the women, and the black curse which have threatened to enslave him. But he does not clearly see that this entire Puritan/anti-Puritan dialectic sets him at odds with the larger reality of life and nature.

The whole of Christmas's reflection on his history is set against the backdrop of the natural world from which he stands apart. Sitting on his cot, he hears "a myriad of sounds . . . —voices, murmurs, whispers: of trees, darkness, earth; people: his own voice; other voices evocative of names and times and places—which he had been conscious of all his life without knowing it, which were his life, thinking *God perhaps and me not knowing that too. . . .*" (98). Christmas is dimly aware that his rebellion has put him at a certain remove from his own life and the larger processes of nature that encompass him. Here, in this fleeting auditory revelation, he hears the sounds of nature and of human existence as part of a single unity, and thinks that this all-embracing reality, rather than the Omnipotent Will of the Puritans, might be God. Joe's meditation brings him as close to an epiphany as he ever comes. He suddenly sees the sentence "*God loves me too*," which means that he has a place in this larger whole which he senses now for the first time. But then he remembers that other God, the one to whom Joanna Burden tried to force him to submit, and he recommits himself to the path of revolt on which he has been set "because she started praying over me" (98).

Joe's alienation from nature finds expression when he strips off his "woman-sewn" undergarment and walks naked in the midnight dew of the Burden property. His popping of the final button which holds his union suit together is meant as a repudiation of the women who have attempted to control him, but his walk through the dew-soaked weeds puts him back in touch with the natural processes which women represent in Faulkner's world. He feels the dew "as he had never felt it before" (100). His stroll is brought to an end, however, when a passing car catches him in its headlights, and he hears the screams of an outraged white woman. The fleeting moment in which Joe is at one with nature despite his hatred of women is cut short, his brief truce with life at an end. He suddenly feels cold. For Joe it "was as though he had merely come there to be present at a finality, and the finality had now occurred and he was free again" (101). He returns to Joanna's window and redresses, symbolically girding up his loins for the final struggle. He is now free, not from his Puritan fate, but from the attraction of nature and the power of life as symbolized by the female. He passes the rest of the night in a stable because horses "are not women. Even a mare horse is a kind of man" (101).

Joe spends the remainder of his life as the observer of actions beyond his control. He has lost his chance at the peace for which he longs. In the chase which follows the murder of Joanna Burden, he remains in the grip of the Puritan superstition that women and blacks are the root of all evil. Like his grandfather before him, he seizes a Negro pulpit in order to curse not only the Negroes with whom his lot has been cast, but God as well. And his distorted relation to nature also finds expression in an obsessive preoccupation with food. Appetite becomes for him entirely a function of the will rather than of instinct, so that he gorges himself on uncooked food. He even loses his moorings in time. It seems to him "that for thirty years he has lived inside an orderly parade of named and numbered days like fence pickets, and that one night he went to sleep and when he waked up he was outside of them" (314). Time becomes a mere mental construction held in place by his will. It is only by accosting strangers and asking them what day it is that he is able to recover any sense of temporal location.

In his final journey through the woods of Yoknapatawpha Joe sees his native country "for the first or the last time," and "the seeing and looking" bring him a strange new kind of peace. But this detached contemplation of nature appears to be only an extreme form of alienation, and he himself realizes that this peace is merely the result of his utter detachment from the world. " 'I dont have to bother about having to eat anymore,' he thinks. 'That's what it is' " (320). His will, in other words, at last simply gives way to despair, and he takes the only straight path which will bring him out of the circle he has been navigating for thirty years. From this moment on it is "as though he had set out and made his plans to passively commit suicide" (419).

VII

Joe's actual death tells us more about the community which sanctions it than it reveals about Joe himself. The final center of action for Christmas's story is the place where his tale first takes shape in the novel, the dark house of Gail Hightower. Hightower's home is the site of Joe's death and the old preacher's reflections provide the fullest assessment of the meaning of Joe's story for the community.

Joe's execution is accomplished by an ill-assorted trio whose motives are decidedly various but who, taken together, represent the forces which have oppressed him from his birth. Doc Hines escapes the confinement imposed upon him by his wife to preach God's hatred of his grandson and to urge the townsfolk to lynch Joe. Though the crowd takes Hines for a madman, his sermon is a grim reminder of the fanatical Puritanism that lies latent those who listen to him. Joe's actual killer represents that same fanaticism, now stripped of its religious pretensions and devoted exclusively to the cult of the community itself. Percy Grimm has been accurately called a proto-Nazi; for him the state commands the sort of ultimate allegiance which Hines grants to his

Calvinistic God, and Grimm sees himself as the avenging angel of the nation as surely as Hines thinks of himself as a new Michael.[12]

When Joe escapes from the authorities he is fleeing from the last of the women who hope to save him so that they can control him. Joe's long-thwarted grandmother, encouraged to act out her own obsession by the birth of Lena's baby and the escape of her vengeful husband, manages to talk her way into Christmas's cell in order to offer him the kind of maternal love he has never known. And his dash to his death must be seen as a refusal not only of the Puritanism which would damn him and of the racist society that will not tolerate him, but also of the women who would love him as well.

While the town is not directly responsible for Joe's death, it stands as an acquiescent chorus in the drama that unfolds on its streets. Like the Puritan obsessives who have warped Joe's psyche, Percy Grimm lives at the moral periphery of Jefferson. Yet, like the Puritans, Grimm is in another sense more faithful to the values of the town than is the town itself. He takes the veterans' parades with which Jefferson glorifies killing and dying for the national cause more seriously than do the veterans themselves, and he forces himself into the ranks of the American Legion. While most of the townsmen grumble that the sheriff cannot be trusted to see that Christmas gets "justice," Grimm actually organizes a local militia to insure that Christmas does not escape. The sheriff and the men who follow Grimm's lead mistrust his zeal, but they allow him to have his way. In the end the residents of the town are horrified by Grimm's sadistic excess, but they recognize that he has acted in their name and out of a passion which they share.

The horror of Joe's death and castration is increased by the fact that Percy Grimm acts as a legally appointed deputy of whose deeds the town itself does not greatly disapprove. As Grimm's last exclamation over the bleeding body of Christmas makes clear, Joe's real crime in the eyes of the community was taking unto himself the sexual prerogative of a white man. The act of vengeance which Grimm performs is not so much punishment for a crime as a denial of Joe's right to exist as a hybrid creature who belongs neither to the white nor the black worlds of Southern society.

While the members of Grimm's vigilante group who witness Christmas's brutal emasculation sense that Christmas's death is somehow a victory for him and an indictment of the town, it is Hightower who sees most clearly the meaning of Joe's death for Jefferson itself, for he comes closest to understanding the connection between the town's religion and Joe's tragedy. As

---

[12]Cf. Brooks, *The Yoknapatawpha Country*, 60–62. In this as in so many cases, Brooks has put his finger on a significant aspect of Faulkner's fiction and drawn the wrong conclusion from it. The horrible truth about Percy Grimm is that his "Storm Trooper" mentality is an exaggerated reflection of his community's morality, not a sign of his alienation from it.

himself a victim of the town's rigid mores, Hightower sees Joe's death as a kind of martyrdom.

On the night before Joe's death, Hightower sits in his study as the Sunday evening service begins in his former church. The music has "a quality stern and implacable, deliberate and without passion so much as immolation, pleading, asking, for not love, nor life, forbidding it to others, demanding in sonorous tones death as though death were a boon. . . . " (347). And as he listens, the defrocked preacher reflects that the religion of his people, like its music, is life-denying; it can tolerate neither "pleasure or catastrophe," and so expends its passion in violence. "Drinking and fighting and praying" are all strategies of violence meant to fend off any emotion which would commit them to respond to life in its fullness. The only possible social relationship which can obtain in such a religion, Hightower sees, is a relation of mutual destruction. "*And so why should not their religion*" Hightower thinks, "*drive them to crucifixion of themselves and one another?*" (347).

Hightower immediately places Joe Christmas in the context of this religion of death. At the end of his meditation he feels the music to be a "dying salute . . . , not to any god but to the doomed man in the barred cell" (348). Not only the Presbyterian church, but all the churches in Jefferson will join in raising the cross upon which Joe Christmas is to be crucified. They will be forced to this action, thinks Hightower, because "to pity him would be to admit selfdoubt and to hope for and need pity themselves" (348). Joe's executioners will slay him "gladly," which is what makes the deed so "terrible." Indeed, as Hightower comes finally to realize, Joe is the perfect Christ figure for this life-denying religion because he has chosen the path of self-destruction which is the secret agenda of all Jefferson life.[13] He is, in other words, not so much a rebel against the faith which has been foisted upon him as he is its unacknowledged champion, for he shares with the Puritans who drive him to suicide a hatred of life, a determination to remain aloof from any emotion which might jeopardize the autonomy of the rational will, and a propensity to use violence as a barrier against the demands of nature.

VIII

Hightower's inability to prevent the crucifixion of Joe Christmas or to reject the religion which demanded it is matched by his inability to grasp the true significance of Lena Grove, the other stranger who disturbs his tranquillity. If Joe is the Christ-figure of the religion of death which provides the

---

[13]. C. Hugh Holman provides a detailed exploration of the analogies between the life of Joe Christmas and that of Christ in "The Unity of Faulkner's *Light in August*," *PMLA*, 73 (1958), 155–66.

groundwork of Southern society, Lena is the goddess of a religion of life. She, like Joe, has broken one of the sexual taboos of Southern society, and like him is on the run. Her "escape," however, is an unhurried affair which takes her beyond the confines of Jefferson. Without being conscious of the fact, she succeeds in transcending the life-denying moralism which finally crushes Christmas. Unmarried and pregnant, without home or family, she suffers neither from self-doubt nor from the animosity of the Puritans. Even the righteous Martha Armstid, who certainly disapproves of Lena's condition, parts with her hard-earned egg money to help Lena on her way.

Byron Bunch, the lone Puritan in the novel who fully appreciates the kind of ingenuous vitality represented by Lena, gives up his job in order to throw in his lot with her. And he prevails upon Hightower to deliver Lena's baby. After the child is born Hightower sees in the birth a sign of the rejuvenation of the land and people which have undergone a symbolic death in the destruction of Joanna Burden's house. He pities the barren woman who died before "luck and life" returned to her ruined acres, as he stands very nearly in the same spot where Joe walked naked in the grass a few days before. It seems to him that he can see and feel "the rich fecund black life of the quarters, the mellow shouts, the presence of fecund women, the prolific naked children in the dust before the doors; and the big house again, noisy, loud with the treble shouts of the generations" (385). But Hightower is not able to sustain this vision; nor is he able to act in accordance with the new values it suggests.

He tries to persuade Lena to turn away from Byron, fearing that Byron has led the sheltered life of a celibate bachelor too long to be able to weather the storms that marriage to a woman as vital and fertile as Lena must bring. He wants to protect Byron in precisely the same way he has sought to protect himself: love refused leaves the perfection of self-absorption intact.

But Lena Grove stands outside the Puritan circle. She is completely caught up in the rhythms of life and love, and she is untouched by those distortions of will which drive the Puritan characters to deal with the world so manipulatively. Indeed, so complete is her participation in nature that she is hardly conscious of herself as a distinct being. She exists in a state of innocence which is prior to the fall of the will into an antagonistic relationship with nature. And thus there is no point of contact between her and the Puritans. Certainly Hightower is unable to reach her, for they dwell in totally different moral spheres.

Light in August ends on the pastoral note of Byron's pursuit of the coy Lena Grove across the hills of Tennessee. Faithful to the mythic mode in which he has cast Lena, Faulkner concludes the novel with what could be called a gently comic meditation on "The Ode to a Grecian Urn."[14] In place of the vicious circle of hatred in which the Puritans seek to assert their alienated wills

---

[14]*Vide* Minter, 20.

against nature and themselves, Byron gives himself over to pursuit, and follows Lena out of love and a new commitment to those natural vitalities which she represents. Their journey is aimless, and Byron in fact must become a "mindless fool" in order to become the lover of this Southern earth goddess.[15] Faulkner leaves the tale of Byron and Lena intentionally incomplete; Byron never achieves his desire. Instead, he attains the state attributed by Keats to the urn-bound Hellenic lovers when he apostrophizes them in the phrase, "for ever wilt thou love, and she be fair."

Byron at least has departed the Puritan circle from which Joe could not escape. But, in allowing him to do so, the novel leaves the tragedy of Joe Christmas unrelieved, since the promised union of lovers who will people the earth anew with their children appears destined to take place outside the bounds of the death-obsessed community. Renewal, it seems, has no place in the world which produced Joe Christmas and Percy Grimm. Faulkner, like Hightower, has not found a way of making any connection between his indictment of the religious foundations of Southern culture and the possibility of rebirth. As Edmund Volpe maintains, *Light in August* deals with extremes, with "resistance and acceptance" of life; "it does not bridge the two."[16]

---

[15]Edmund Volpe, *A Reader's Guide to William Faulkner* (New York: Farrar, Strauss, and Giroux, 1964), 160–61.

[16]Volpe, 160.

CHAPTER 4

THE IRONIC MYTH: *GO DOWN, MOSES*

I

Go Down, Moses stands as the culmination of Faulkner's efforts to come to terms with the romance of innocence, and as such it represents the climax of his religious critique of Southern culture. Faulkner often said that he was trying "to write it all on the head of a pin," to tell one story perfectly. And in this work he finally realized his highest achievement in clarity of expression.[1]

It will be the burden of this chapter to demonstrate that, while *Go Down, Moses* is not Faulkner's richest book, it articulates most clearly the conception of human life on which all his other books depend. It lacks the scope and passion of much of his earlier work, but it exemplifies a coherence and mastery which he would never again quite reach.

In *Light in August,* Faulkner lays bare the religious foundations of Southern culture. From the implicit attack on the ethical presuppositions of his region in *The Sound and the Fury* and *Absalom, Absalom* he turns here to the religious roots of those values in what he calls "Puritanism." But, as we have seen, the Puritan myth which Faulkner indicts is supplanted in the novel only by the escapist pastoralism he builds around Lena Grove. He condemns Southern culture as at bottom life-denying, but he sees no alternative to its religion of death except that of a kind of ingenuous vitalism.

---

[1]*Vide* R.W.B. Lewis, "The Hero in the New World: William Faulkner's *The Bear*," *Kenyon Review,* XIII: 4 (Autumn 1951), 641–60, and Millgate, *The Achievement of William Faulkner,* for example.

Faulkner's exploration of the Southern character moves into a new phase, however, in *Go Down, Moses,* for in Isaac McCaslin he creates a character who combines the moral sensitivity of a Quentin Compson or a Gail Hightower with the sympathy for nature that marks a Lena Grove. Like Quentin and Hightower, Ike is the eldest son of an aristocratic house and is highly conscious of the burden of his heritage. On the other hand, he is most at home in the natural world from which Faulkner's other hyperconscious aristocrats are alienated. The big woods of *Go Down, Moses* are indeed a kind of Eden that is described in the majestic cadences of the Old Testament.[2] The formative events of Ike's life take place here, rather than in the house or town which is the usual site of Faulkner's aristocratic dramas. But the worlds of nature and society are not divorced in this work as they are in his earlier fiction.

II

Michael Millgate is entirely convincing when he argues that *Go Down, Moses* should be read as a unified novel rather than a collection of stories.[3] Critics have correctly seen that "The Bear" is the centerpiece of the volume, and that Ike McCaslin is its most significant figure; so I shall treat them as the center towards which the whole of the novel gravitates. Ike is the high priest who presides over the ritual drama described in "The Bear," and it is the story told there which provides the mythic core at the heart of the entire book.

The first and most crucial question to ask of "The Bear" concerns the relation between the two stories it interweaves.[4] On the one hand, there is the tale of Ike's initiation into the priesthood of the hunt which has as its central event the slaying of Old Ben. On the other hand there is the story of Ike's awakening to the sins of his fathers and his rejection of his patrimony. The first story takes place in the wilderness, the second in the civilized world of the town into which Ike was born.

Clearly, these two worlds are different and, in a sense, even polar opposites. To put the difference most sharply (but too crudely), the forest represents nature, the town culture. The wood is nature in its primal state, unaltered by human artifice. The timber has never been cut, the rivers are undammed. It is a realm inhabited by untamed creatures and presided over by

---

[2] R.W.B. Lewis does an estimable job of capturing this dimension of "The Bear" in the aforementioned article.

[3] *The Achievement of William Faulkner.*

[4] Critics have long been fascinated with the relation between the fourth section of "The Bear" and the hunting story which surrounds it. See, for example, Lawrance Thompson, *William Faulkner: An Introduction and Interpretation.*

forces which man does not control. Sam Fathers greets with reverence the great animal spirits of the forest: the snake, the unearthly buck, the awesome bear. When these mysterious creatures make their appearance, the event is charged with meaning for the human beholder. Ike, for example, is able to see Old Ben only after he has gone into the deepest part of the forest, laid down his compass and watch, and found the three-toed print which is the bear's signature. Encountering the bear is for Ike an experience of the *mysterium tremendum et fascinans,* in Rudolf Otto's phrase.[5] The wood is a realm charged with spiritual power.

The human activity which takes place in the big wood is ritually controlled. Every member of the hunting party has a carefully defined role outside which he never steps. The structure of this tiny society is hierarchical, but the hierarchy is different from that of town society. Outside the forest, Sam Fathers is a half-caste handyman; in the woods he is a priest, the only man fully initiated into the mystery of the wilderness. It is Sam who insures not only that game is hunted successfully, but that it is slain correctly, according to the "yearly pageant rite."

Sam exemplifies the aristocracy of merit which prevails in the woods. Though bloodlines influence abilities in this world (Sam, though half-Indian and part Negro, is descended from kings on both sides), it is achievement which determines one's place in the social structure. Another feature of the hunting camp is its democratic attitude toward property. The best shot rides the best mount, no matter to whom the animal belongs. Most important, Major De Spain only nominally owns the woods, for the forest is outside any human jurisdiction and is not something to be possessed.

Town society, like the hunting party, is hierarchically arranged. But here birth, not ability, is the determining factor. Race is the great dividing line. And nowhere does birth play a larger role than in ownership of property for one's status is determined by one's possessions. In place of ritual, which serves the hunters as a means of mediation between the human and the natural spheres, the town relies on manners to control the forms of interaction among people. And the social conventions which make up the system of manners are designed to protect the arbitrary class structure of town culture. Nowhere is the force of manners more apparent than in the interchanges between black and white members of the McCaslin clan which take place over the plantation ledger-book. In one particularly striking series of encounters, the illiterate Roskus comes as he annually does, to stand before the book that records the slowly accumulating price of his freedom. Despite the fact that he cannot understand a word which is recorded in the book, Roskus must go through the

---

[5]*The Idea of the Holy,* trans. by John W. Harvey (New York: Oxford University Press, 1923).

motions which the system of manners has established, just as Ike must employ a certain ritual in his dealings with the natural order. The almost magical relation in the woods between man and the natural powers is in the town supplanted by the nearly mechanical relation between labor and balance sheets. In the forest a natural hierarchy reigns, whereas in town it is an arbitrary hierarchy based primarily upon color that prevails. The wilderness belongs to no one, but in town land is neatly parceled and deeded. There are no women in the big woods society, yet the town could not function without them.

This dichotomy between town and woods, culture and nature, is at the heart of *Go Down, Moses,* and indeed of Faulkner's whole fictional world. We have seen one version of it in Faulkner's treatment of "the doomed little girl with muddy drawers" in *The Sound and the Fury,* another in the contrast between Lena Grove and Joe Christmas in *Light in August.* "Was," the first story in *Go Down, Moses,* is set before the Sutpenesque backdrop of the plantation in its raw youth, where the distinction between culture and nature is still blurred. But here already we witness a hunt where the "game" which is the hunters' quarry is not an animal, but a black man. The rigid and arbitrary social hierarchy of color is at odds with the frontier democracy which has the masters of the McCaslin plantation living in a cabin and their slaves settled in the big house. Women, who are carefully excluded from the male paradise of the big woods and the bachelor preserve of Uncle Buck and Uncle Buddy, make their appearance in the persons of Miss Sophonsiba and the granddaughter of James Beauchamp. When they do emerge (most powerfully in "Delta Autumn"), the inherent tensions between the worlds of town and woods become irresolvable.

Despite the differences between them, town and wilderness are connected in the minds of those who live in both spheres. In fact, the hunters of "The Bear" assume that the values which regulate life in the big woods should carry over directly to town life. Ike's initiation into the circle of hunters is also his initiation into manhood. The older men believe that, in learning to be a good woodsman, Ike is also preparing for his adult responsibilities and for the position he will hold in the Jefferson community. Their attitude toward town and wilderness, and their assessment of Ike's place in the two, are expressed by General Compson when Cass Edmonds, Ike's older cousin and guardian, refuses to let Ike stay with the ailing Sam Fathers after the climactic hunt:

> And you shut up Cass. . . . You've got one foot straddled into a farm and the other foot straddled into a bank; you aint even got a good handhold where this boy was already an old man long before you damn Sartorises and Edmondses invented farms and

banks to keep yourselves from having to find out what this boy was born knowing . . . maybe by God that's the why and wherefore of farms and banks (250–51).[6]

In this passage both the difference and the connection between town and forest are emphasized. Cass has given himself so completely to town life that he is estranged from the more important reality of the woods. But the General believes that the humanly structured order of the town should reflect the values of the natural order. General Compson praises Ike for his expertise in the ways of the woods, and implies that because of it Ike has a better grasp on the real foundations of human existence. Yet in this instance (as in many future ones), Ike's devotion to the wilderness leads him to neglect his responsibilities to the world of farms and banks.

It is significant that General Compson's comment on the relationship between wilderness and town is focused on Ike McCaslin. "The Bear" is after all Ike's story; it takes its shape from the choice he must make between what he perceives as the conflicting values of town and woods. What we learn about the two societies we must discover through him.

The two crucial episodes in Ike's life are his initiation into the priesthood of the hunt and his refusal of his patrimony. Both are complex events wherein the culture/nature theme of *Go Down, Moses* is filtered through the consciousness of Faulkner's most enlightened idealist.

III

Ike's refusal of the McCaslin plantation is in fact an expression of how deeply he is troubled by the tension he feels between life in the woods and life in the world of farms and banks. This becomes apparent when, just after turning twenty-one, he explains to his older cousin Cass why he can't accept his grandfather's legacy. He argues that he cannot inherit the land because it was not "owned" by his grandfather or anyone else. Citing Genesis, he claims that man's role on the earth is that of steward and communicant, not owner and sole proprietor. Man was created, Ike says,

not to hold for himself and his descendants inviolable title forever, generation after generation, to the oblongs and squares of the earth, but to hold the earth mutual and intact in the communal anonymity of brotherhood . . . (257).

The contrast Ike insists upon between the ideal and the actual is the difference between forest and town as they are portrayed in "The Bear." He realizes that his stand is idealistic and that in the eyes of everyone except himself and God his grandfather did own the land. Nevertheless, he is convinced

---

[6]*Go Down, Moses* (New York: Random House, 1942; Vintage Books rprt., 1973). All page references are to this volume, and will be included in the body of the chapter.

that possessing property destroys the communion of man and nature and God. By dividing the earth into oblongs and squares, we destroy the primordial unity of life.

The divisive nature of property is most evident in the institution of slavery. The rift in the human community is obvious when one class holds another as chattels. Ike reflects long and hard on the history of slavery in his family. As he reads the account books which chronicle the story, he comes to see slavery as a curse which haunts the lives of the white and black McCaslins at every turn. Slavery is a particularly noxious form of the sin of ownership; it institutionalizes the lines of status which mark yet another divergence of town life from the wilderness code. The natural aristocracy which forms the basis of the hunting camp hierarchy is latent in town society, but racism undermines it.

The history of the McCaslin family is replete with examples of Negroes who are as noble of bearing and as courageous and clever as old Carothers McCaslin himself. Indeed, Faulkner makes this equality explicit in his characterization of Lucas McCaslin in "The Fire and the Hearth." But the racial system does not allow these people to take their rightful place in the social hierarchy. They are oppressed by "the curse of [the] fathers, the haughty ancestral pride based not on any value, but on an accident of geography, stemmed not from courage and honor but from wrong and shame . . . " (111). Ike admires the daring of the young Lucas, who on the morning of his twenty-first birthday appears at Ike's doorstep and demands his inheritance. And he is struck by the pride and perseverance which prompt a slave in his father's time to refuse the gift of freedom in order that he might earn it with hard labor instead. But in a racist society such virtues go unacknowledged. Ike is perfectly aware that scoundrels are to be found on both sides of the color line; but what distresses him is the false assumption that race determines merit. In his view, those born to lead and those born to follow cannot be separated by race. The town measures worth according to this bogus standard, but it does not prevail in the woods.

The section of "The Bear" which relates Ike's decision to relinquish his patrimony also draws out the difference between ritual and manners. Both conventions serve to mediate among individuals or between man and nature, but manners produce only the semblance of the mediation which ritual actually supplies. In the forest Ike is marked with the blood of his first kill, symbolizing his union with the buck and with the community of hunters. The chief symbol of what I am calling manners is the ledger, which falsely relates white to black in the language of balance sheets.[7] Again the source of the difference

---

[7] By "manners" I mean the cultural code of behavior that regulates social behavior in a given society. It becomes a pejorative term in my treatment of *Go Down, Moses* only because

is the concept of property. The white McCaslins do not, on Ike's analysis, own their slaves or the labor of their tenants, and so the ledger cannot properly mediate between the two groups. The ritual of Ike's initiation reveals that, though boy, buck, and hunters have different functions, they are each part of a single community held together by mutual respect. Similarly, the ledger records the sum of property transactions on the plantation, and binds together all the inhabitants in a single network. Yet the premise of the second system is false, according to Ike, and so while the plantation is an economic unit composed of humans, animals, and land, it is not a community.

Manners operate in a more conventional form in the encounter between Cass and the Negro who marries Fonsiba. Ike watches as Cass bristles at the impudence of the Negro who refuses to address the white man as "sir." According to the code by which the plantation operates, the speech of Negroes and whites is supposed to reflect the inferior social position of the one and the superiority of the other. The Negro violates this code and so creates hostility between himself and Cass. In the absence (or rejection) of prescribed manners, mediation breaks down.

Yet, even when the characters remain within the code of manners, no true mediation takes place; the code is based on false values which disregard the dignity of the inferior class. Although he allows his wife to go, Lucas Beauchamp rightly feels insulted, for example, when in "The Fire and the Hearth" Zack Edmonds takes her into his house as housekeeper and nurse after Louisa Edmonds dies in childbirth. Zack's action lies within the prerogatives which the code of manners gives him, but Lucas is stripped of his dignity when he is deprived of his wife, and it is no wonder that he eventually comes within an ace of killing Zack.

Having recognized the guilt of his forebears, Ike searches in vain for a means to recompense the black McCaslins for the wrongs their white cousins have committed against them, and to bring together the two branches of his family to proper relation. But the means available to him do not truly atone for the sins of his fathers. Though he scrupulously gives each of the black descendants his or her share of the McCaslin inheritance, neither the money nor the act of giving it reconciles the parties. Just as the property relation poisoned the life of a human community in the beginning, so it is an inadequate antidote after the fact. Ike's dissatisfaction with town values and his failure

---

it formalizes the ascription of status on the basis of property and race. I am not opposed (nor is Faulkner) to manners as such, but both of us believe that the values which this set of manners protect are false values. The distinction I make here between ritual and manners is intended only to illustrate the difference between woods and town in this novel, and cannot be pushed beyond that application. A large portion of what I call the ritual of the woods could fairly be called a different set of manners, but I have been unable to arrive at a more satisfactory set of terms to draw out the real differences between the two societies.

to amend the family's wrongs within its social structure are largely due to the inability of manners to provide ritual mediation.

Ike also finds that relations between the sexes are sullied by ownership of property. Comparison between the codes of the wilderness and the town seems impossible in this connection since there are no women in the hunting camp. But if we take the woods to be an Eden which represents the ideal, a startling conclusion follows. In the ideal society there are no relations between the sexes; sex differences are eliminated, for the perfect community contains only one sex. The difference between woods and town on the matter of sex is absolute. This observation raises the question of whether sex itself is inherently corrupt, as the other elements of town life seem to be. Ike's own experience suggests that it is.

Ike certainly has no built-in bias against sexual relations. He falls in love with a woman and marries her. But his wife virtually cancels their marriage when Ike refuses to claim his inheritance. She directly ties the sex act to ownership of property, telling him at the crucial moment in their marriage that if Ike will not take possession of the land that is rightfully his she will never sleep with him again. When she makes love to him for the last time, it is in the attempt to make Ike change his mind. Sex is for her a bargaining tool in a contest of wills.

After his wife's ultimatum, Ike lives without female companionship, and in effect becomes a celibate. This fact, along with the total absence of women in the woods, suggests that sexual relations have no place in Eden. Since in Ike's experience sexual relations inevitably degenerate into power struggles, they cannot be part of the pure life he would lead.

There is at least one reason for believing that the connection between sex and property is not accidental but essential. Sex produces children who must be cared for, and in town society only property can provide security for them. Ike's wife is clearly thinking along these lines when, after first seducing him, she says, "If this dont get you that son you talk about, it wont be mine . . ." (315). She is not, as some have claimed, merely trying to force Ike to elevate their social position by taking the plantation.[8] She is concerned for the future of their children. Her logic seems to be that, if Ike will not provide for his children, he should not become a father.

This line of reasoning is the female counterpart to the rationale which permits Ike's grandfather to commit his outrage against his slaves. Women are not alone in using sex as an expression of power in *Go Down, Moses*. The darkest blot on his heritage to be found in the ledgers comes to light when Ike discovers that his grandfather not only used a married slave as his mistress

---

[8]*Vide* Brooks's interpretation of the motives of Ike's wife and his comment on Andrew Lytle's "Faulkner's *A Fable*," *Sewanee Review, 63* (1955), 127–28.

but slept with the daughter who was their offspring, causing the mother to drown herself in despair. Since he is the master of boundless property, Old Carothers may, according to the unstated Southern code, father as many children as he likes on any of the women in his domain.

Ike's *de facto* celibacy, though itself unchosen, is an inevitable consequence of his decision to renounce his patrimony. Ike's wife correctly intuits that his rejection of the values which form the basis of town society means that he may not be expected to maintain himself successfully in its commercial life. So she refuses to cohabit with him, fearing that his progeny will be penniless. And the logic of the situation is clear: to repudiate property is to lose sexual rights and is thus to be childless. In short, by breaking the chain that links the McCaslins to the plantation, Ike ends the line of the McCaslins. By separating himself from his forebears, he also cuts himself off from his descendants.

Ike's decision to refuse his inheritance thus lands him in a paradoxical position. His action is meant to atone for the sins of his fathers and so to rectify the flaws of a social order which has succumbed to the temptation of property. But so vital is the property relation to town society that to renounce it entirely is to exile oneself altogether. Instead of reforming the world of farms and banks, Ike has removed himself from its on-going life.

IV

The dilemma in which Ike finds himself is puzzling in light of the clear conviction of the other white hunters that life in the town and life in the woods are complementary. Ike's decision on his twenty-first birthday suggests that, on the contrary, the norms of the two communities represent an either/or alternative. Is he falsely interpreting the values of the woods? Much is at stake here, for, if Ike is correct, it would appear that Faulkner has once again juxtaposed a mythic idealization of nature with an ironic indictment of culture. But we must at least entertain the possibility that the hunters' intuition is borne out, and that the town community does indeed reflect that of the woods. If such is the case, then here, for the first time in Faulkner's work, there is a point of connection between the previously contrary modes of his art. We must ask whether Ike's paradise does not harbor its own serpent. Does the way of the big woods really represent an ideal alternative to the deeply flawed human structures of the town, or are the seeds of corruption also present in the wilderness itself?

The answers to these questions lie within the tale of the killing of Old Ben. When Ike is forced to interpret events in the life of the town, he invariably draws on what he has learned in the forest. The effect of this dual focus is to make us believe that town society must be understood as having its origins in the life of the big woods, which logically and historically precedes it. Man in the forest is in his primal state; town society springs from these origins. Furthermore, the mythic elements we have noted in the hunting story underscore this distinction between original and derivative societies. It would seem, therefore, that Ike's procedure is correct, and that we too must look to the hunting story to explain later events in town. But in adopting Ike's method we need not accept his interpretation of wilderness experience. The story places Ike himself in a frame which discloses Faulkner's larger vision. What we may hope to find within the hunting tale is a mythic core which puts Ike and the whole of human existence into comprehensive perspective.

In "The Bear," Faulkner has for the first time in his career used the mythic mode of his art to complement the ironic, rather than to counter it. Whereas Faulkner had previously employed myth as an escape from the bleak world which the realistic dimension of his art revealed, here myth explains social reality. The hunting story allows us to understand the history of Jefferson at a depth which would otherwise be impossible; conversely, the historical dimension of the narrative enables us to interpret the myth. In "The Bear," myth and history are integrally related. The barriers which formerly separated them have been struck down.

Despite its mythic elements, the story maintains its basic realistic stance throughout. Nowhere in the work do we discover myth in its purest form; not even the hunting tale takes place *in illo tempore,* to be retold in the contrasting historical present of the town. Instead, we find throughout a wealth of detail that reproduces the everyday life of temporally conditioned characters. The forest is itself mortal, and at the end of "The Bear" it suffers an actual demise. Yet the tone of the hunting tale suggests that the events it records are fraught with larger implications. In order to grasp the import of Faulkner's juxtaposition of town and woods, we must look for the myth that he has implanted in the events of the bear hunt and interpret it in the frame of the realistic detail in which it is embedded.

Among the characters involved in the myth of the hunt Sam Fathers serves as a kind of priest, and any thorough account of the mythic core of the hunting tale must begin with him. When the story begins he is already initiated into the mysteries of the big woods. It is he who trains young hunters and who decides when and how game is to be hunted.

Ike and Boon have a special relationship with Sam. Ike, the better qualified to assume Sam's role, serves him as an apprentice or novice; in fact, as his name suggests, Sam is something like Ike's spiritual father. Boon is Sam's servant. He tends the dog Sam has trained; he has a natural affinity for the forest but lacks the skill and intelligence of Sam and Ike. Both Ike and Boon in some sense serve Sam Fathers, yet Ike is cast as reflective, conscientious, and skillful while Boon is spontaneous, carefree, and bumbling. When Major

De Spain sends Boon into Memphis for whisky, he sends Ike with him to insure that some of the liquor will return to camp. Ike acts to restrain the unbridled Boon, and to channel his energy into productive activity. Their relationship is in fact similar to that between Sam and Lion. Lion is pure destructive force; Sam cleverly shapes him into a useful hunter.

The two heroic animals also have much in common. Old Ben is the "head bear" presented as the god of the wood. No dog can hold him and no bullet can slay him. He is an enigma that the hunters cannot penetrate. Lion, too is identified with elemental forces. Before Sam captures him, the hunters mistake him for Old Ben. Only the bear, they believe, is capable of killing a colt at its dam's side as Lion has done. Even in captivity Lion is indomitable. He is never tamed; his ferocity is simply held in check until it can be unleashed on Old Ben. Lion and Old Ben are pitted against each other in the hunt, where they take on allegorical significance: fierce destructive power assaults the mighty god of the forest.

A one-sided love affair develops between Boon and Lion. Boon sleeps with Lion in the camp; and when Sam Fathers and Lion both fall after the slaying of Old Ben, Boon shocks Ike and Major De Spain by demanding a horse to fetch the doctor—not for Sam, but for Lion. Boon, the spontaneous man of passion, is thus the lover of the dog who represents pure destructive force.

The final significant relationship which must be noted is the bond between Sam, Ike, and Old Ben. Sam and Ike, in a sense priests who serve the god of the wood, are also plotters of his death. Ike undergoes an ordeal in order to gain sight of the bear. In this first encounter, Ike stands before Old Ben in awe, having stripped himself of all human possessions. The second time he faces the bear he has his gun in his hands, yet he does not shoot. Nevertheless, Ike and Sam make it their chief business to bring the long pursuit of the bear to a successful conclusion which can only mean his death. As we shall soon see more fully, the function of these priests in the myth is to preside over the ritual slaying of the god whom they serve, but not to kill him themselves.

The myth, in other words, is a narrative that develops the theme of man's relationship to nature, and it discloses man's attitude toward nature to be one that is bifurcated. On the one hand, he identifies with nature and seeks to maintain communion with it; on the other hand, he desires to subjugate it. These conflicting desires are represented by Sam and Ike on the one side, and by Boon on the other. Though Sam and Ike acknowledge the need to hunt the bear, communion is their chief aim. And thus it is left to Boon to make the kill.

Boon represents in its purest form the desire to subjugate nature. But his role in the myth is far from simple. For though he is himself animal-like and thus in one sense the most "natural" of the hunters, his very brutishness drives him to slay the god of nature. So it appears that man at his most instinctual is most fierce in his desire to assert himself against the natural world.

Boon's case is further complicated by the fact that it is both love and bloodlust that drive him to thrust the knife into Old Ben's heart. He leaps astride the bear only when he sees that Lion is about to lose his life. Is Boon protecting Lion or simply eager to share in the kill? Faulkner suggests that Boon slays Ben for both reasons. The sexual overtones in the encounter are difficult to ignore. We know that Boon has been abnormally devoted to Lion. He sleeps with him and cares for him as a town wife might her husband. And the death scene on the river bank is portrayed as if it were the occasion of a brutal sexual coupling where Boon's long courtship of Lion is finally consummated on the bear. When the three rush together, embrace as one, then fall apart when the knife pierces the bear's heart, it is as though we have witnessed a lover's tryst in the woods. The result of this coupling is not conception, however, but death. Only Boon survives. He has conquered, but also destroyed. Lion and Ben are transformed from mysterious centers of the life force which animates nature to mere carcasses, just as the big woods itself will soon be transformed into stacks of lumber.

Sam and Ike witness this bloody tryst as interested observers. They preside over the killing as men of consciousness (in contrast to Boon, who acts out of instinctual lust) who insure that Ben's death is ritually correct. After the death scene—in the course of which Sam is fatally stricken by a stroke—it is Ike who leads the procession back to camp and insists on remaining with Sam, despite the doctor's erroneously optimistic prognosis. He has assumed Sam's role as priest of the hunt, though now that the god of the forest is dead we realize that Ike will be the last of his order.

In the myth of the hunt, the desire to slay and the desire to commune with nature stand as unreconciled opposites. Consciousness is divorced from instinct; Sam and Ike must watch, Boon must kill. This separation of powers does not mean, however, that either can function without the other. Without Boon there would have been no kill; without Sam and Ike, Boon would never have arrived at his tryst. Consciousness without the will to subjugate is impotent; passion without consciousness is ineffectual.

If our reading of the sexual drama at the hunt's climax is correct, the sex drive is yet another instance of the will to subjugate and slay. Boon plays an androgynous role in the affair, caring for Lion as a wife would, but mounting the bear and wielding the phallic knife as though he were the male lover in a brutal coupling. In both cases, the will to subjugate is dominant. Boon loves Lion for his fierceness and independence, yet he attempts to domesticate him. Both Lion and Boon mount the bear in order to vanquish it. The female sexual instinct is to rob the male of his independence; that of the male is to dominate the female. In both cases the sex drive is an expression of the will to subjugate. True union or communion is impossible. "Love" is actually a struggle of wills bent on victory.

As the hunt-myth suggests, man's relation to nature is adversarial. Human nature itself reflects this state of affairs. Consciousness, the attribute which distinguishes man from the animals, is sundered from instinct. He thus lives in tension with himself. Through consciousness, man longs both to be reunited with nature and to subjugate it. The desire for mastery arises from the instincts themselves, though it can be fully realized only by consciousness. It is thus consciousness which empowers the will to dominate nature. But in separating himself from nature, man also isolates himself from other human persons and turns sex, which is "intended" to be an instrument of human communion into merely another battleground of wills.

How, then, can consciousness mediate between the desire for mastery and the longing for union? The need to reconcile these two desires raises what are quite literally life-and-death issues. Man is forced to "kill" nature for two reasons. First, he must turn nature to his use for physical survival. Without the meat of animals and the produce of farms, he could not live. But to subjugate nature in this way is to kill it—to erase its distinctiveness. Moreover, the very processes of consciousness objectify nature. To be conscious means to recognize the distance between oneself and nature. Complete unification with nature is possible only in death, when consciousness ceases to separate the self from its external environment.

Mediation between man and nature is possible, then, only if there is present in nature a spirit corresponding to human consciousness. Ike and Sam act out of the conviction that there is such a spiritual reality and that through it man can both exist apart from nature and be reconciled to it. For them, ritual is the means whereby this reconciliation takes place. In "Delta Autumn" Ike articulates the attitude wherewith one should approach the animal he has killed: "I slew you; my bearing must not shame your quitting life. My conduct forever onward must become your death . . . " (351). Ike assumes that the animal is enspirited by a larger life force which includes the hunter's consciousness. That spirit is accessible; acting within the ritual code, the hunter may slay game without violating nature or divorcing himself from it.

But, in the myth, this strategy seems not to succeed, for Boon kills Old Ben out of blind passion; his bearing remains completely unaltered after Ben's death. Whatever ritual reconciliation takes place is strictly Ike's affair. Though Boon operates within the context provided by Sam and Ike, the difference between the attitudes of Ike and Boon is too great for the ritual to overcome it. Natural and conscious man remain segregated; the contrast between the bloody killing and the later procession-cum-funeral is so stark that the need for harmony between man and nature is left unsatisfied despite Ike's efforts.

The aftermath of the events chronicled in the myth support our negative conclusion. After the hunt, Major De Spain sells the forest. Soon the loggers move in, turning the forest to lumber as surely as the steady working of Boon's knife finds out the heart of the bear, and nature becomes an object of subjugation rather than communion. In the episode with which "The Bear" closes, as Ike makes his private meditation at the graves of Sam, Lion, and Old Ben, the spirit of the woods appears, this time in the guise of a snake. This climactic scene is shattered in the next instant: Ike notices that Boon is seated under a nearby tree which teems with squirrels and that he is hammering in frustration at his jammed shotgun. "Get out of here!" he yells at Ike. "Dont touch a one of them! They're mine!" (331). The clear implication is that human rapacity has won out over the desire for communion. In the heart of the big woods lurks the same fatal flaw in man's relation to nature that poisons the life of the town. As in the earlier scene when Old Ben meets his violent end, Ike in this instance is again the observer of Boon's destructive passion. Only this time, Ike is unable to provide even the semblance of ritual reconciliation between the desire to slay and respect for the spirit which unites man with the natural order.

V

The myth which lies at the heart of "The Bear" places Ike's rejection of his patrimony in a new light. From Ike's own perspective, the wilderness way of life represents an ideal by which town society may be called to account. At every point Ike sees his decision as a choice between the values of the woods and those of town society. He must accept ownership of the land or act on the conviction that the earth is for the use of all men. By becoming head of a plantation he would tacitly accept a racist system which violates the natural hierarchy of merit that operates in the hunting camp. Because he cannot conscientiously live by the rule of the ledger book, Ike is finally forced to adopt the sexless celibacy of the woods rather than the role of husband and father he desires. In his experience, sexual relations are governed by yet another set of conventions which promise communion but actually mask the conflict of selfish wills. Thus, Ike is driven to forsake his place in the larger society in the name of the higher morality of the wilderness.

But the myth of the hunt, as Faulkner presents it, undercuts Ike's interpretation of the wilderness experience. His rejection of his patrimony is based on a distinction which the myth calls into question. Town society, he thinks, operates according to a corrupt version of those virtues which he identifies with those of the big woods. Yet the myth of the hunt shows that the fatal flaw is at the very heart of Eden; the injustices from which Ike recoils lie at the root of all human existence.

Ike's role in town society is essentially the one he occupies in the myth. He is the priest, the man of conscience who attempts to expiate the sins committed by a consciousness-heightened will to power. He refuses to be the hunter in town society; that is, he will not let himself exercise the desire to subjugate by owning property. Instead, he seeks ritually to purify the land which his grandfather defiled by taking possession of it. He attempts to make amends for the wrongs his white family has perpetrated against its black members, and hopes by relinquishing the land to restore it to its pristine state. He is mistaken in his belief that such a reconciliation is possible, just as he is wrong in thinking that he and Sam have harmonized the bloodlust of Lion and Boon with the spirit of nature. The Negroes refuse or misuse the money he gives them; the plantation stays in the hands of his cousin Cass, who runs it as it has always been operated.

On the other hand, Ike denies the legitimacy of the very actions necessary to sustain human existence. His longing for communion leads him to deny all self-assertion. He will not shoot the bear, though he wants to do so and does not question the necessity of killing him. He refuses his inheritance, though this action means at once that he is losing his chance to improve the lot of the tenants and that the line of his own family will end. Ike's wife correctly sees that his refusal of the land is a rejection of the course of action necessary to sustain human life. It is altogether fitting that he should have no children. Ike's idealism, though admirable, is based on a false reading of both natural and social realities. Life in the woods operates according to the same values as town society, but Ike has misread the lessons to be learned there.

The greatest irony of "The Bear" arises from the fact that its myth confirms the values of the town as the only ones by which society can function. Property is simply a sophisticated system for expressing the will to subjugate. In the woods this desire takes the form of the lust for the kill. This primal urge is an instinct common to man as such. Furthermore, it is necessary for survival. The institution of property makes systematic what in the woods is spontaneous. There is no essential difference between Boon's killing the bear and Major De Spain's selling the camp. Unless man asserts himself against nature, mastering it to his will and use, he can neither be human nor survive. Yet this action cuts him off from communion with nature.

The relation between man and nature also obtains within the strictly human economy. Human life consists of instinctual and reflective elements which are never unified. Consciousness may raise the power of the will to dominate, or it may turn against that urge in the form of conscience; but consciousness itself always interjects distance between the self as subject and the self as object. In the myth this distance is that between Boon on one side of the river in the act of killing the bear and Ike watching from the other side. On the plantation, the span is measured by the length of the trek the field hand makes to stand before the ledger in the farm store. The very distinction between men as hunters and men as farmers and bankers is but a manifestation of the division of instinct and consciousness that human beings carry everywhere with them.

The harsh objectification of persons which Ike notes in racial and sexual relationships is a result of this inevitable split. The roles which society forces upon individuals never reflect their personhood. The Negro is not simply an object worth so much in the coin of work; men and women are not merely buyers and sellers of sexual pleasure who want nothing more than orgasms or plantations from each other. By the same token, Cass and Major De Spain are more than coldly shrewd businessmen who are expert in society's power game. The persons who reside behind these masks cannot be fully embodied in any role. Consciousness, the faculty which makes these masks false, prevents any role from accurately reflecting the whole of the self.

It is no wonder, then, that ritual and manners fail to reconcile persons to persons or human beings to nature. As we have seen, Ike's attempt to cancel the moral breach between the white and black sides of his family fails because the only means of mediation he has lies in such a manipulation of property as that which originally caused the division. But he is no more successful in the woods. Boon's and Lion's impassioned destructiveness is not redeemed by the ritual which surrounds it. After the hunt, the god of the wood is vanquished, and the forest disappears.

Here we have come to the central flaw in Ike's conception of the world. The mysterious spirit which animates nature and fills human consciousness with longing is not accessible through ritual or any other human means. It may or may not make itself known to those who are open to its approach. Those moments of grace where consciousness is at one with life come always in the midst of that striving and essential alienation which is man's fate. The spirit of the big woods, like the truth which Cass believes Keats to have described in "Ode on a Grecian Urn," is an object of human pursuit which can never be captured, and which may, in fact, be an illusion.

Ike is not willing to accept the essentially tragic state of human existence. The real tragedy of the hunt-myth is not that the affront against nature leads to dire consequences for man but that there is no return to Eden after the fall. No act of repudiation, no matter how complete, can ever heal the breach between man and nature established by consciousness and the will to power.

What does remain after the hunt is conscience—the sense of loss and guilt which consciousness feels as a result of alienation. Knowledge of one's estrangement, and the unwillingness to make one's peace with it, is in Faulkner's world the highest achievement of moral man. Ike's mistake lies in the belief that the war against alienation can ever be won. The trap into which he falls is the notion that he can escape the tragic fatality against which he would rebel. By becoming exclusively a man of conscience, Ike contracts out of the human condition and thus condemns himself in the end to ineffectualness.

The irony of his position is captured in the conclusion of "Delta Autumn," after women for the first time have become the subject of the male conversation of the hunting camp. At the climax of the story, Roth's lover bursts in on the sleeping Uncle Ike. To his later shame the startled old man immediately blurts out, "You're a nigger!" (361). Despite his own past efforts to negate the sins of his fathers, he has not succeeded in uprooting even his own prejudice. He is surprised and offended to discover that Roth's beloved is a Negro. When the complexities of town society confront him in the wilderness where he has hitherto thought to escape them, Ike in the event fails to prove faithful to the wilderness virtues. Once he recovers from the shock of the encounter he suggests to the woman that, if she will marry a black man, in time she will forget Roth. But the daughter of Tennie's Jim counters that "you dont remember anything you ever knew or felt or even heard about love . . . " (363). And she speaks more truly perhaps than she knows, for Ike's detachment from life has made it impossible for him to comprehend human passion.

Then, in a gesture pregnant with meaning, Ike gives to this woman for her son the silver hunting horn which symbolizes life in the big woods. And the gift of the horn is his acknowledgement of the child which Roth has denied. Though this gesture does not mitigate the tragedy which has evoked it, it is at least a protest against the inhumanity of which all the McCaslins are guilty. Ike is an idealist whose vision is flawed by his inability to accept the inescapably tragic quality of human life. But from Faulkner's perspective, his is a noble failure.

VI

Faulkner's ambivalent attitude toward his protagonist is a reflection of the ironic myth he fashions in *Go Down, Moses*. Ike's attempt to amend the ethical flaw in his tradition fails not only because he has misread the lessons of the woods, but because in Faulkner's view morality itself is doomed to failure. The myth of "The Bear" is ironic because it calls into question the efficacy of the very rituals it sponsors. Indeed, the final import of the hunting story is the denial of the very reconciliation between man and nature that the ritual of the great hunt is supposed to effect. The difference, in other words, between woods and town is finally annulled, and the "flaw" of human consciousness is shown to be present in both societies.

Like the epiphanies Ike experiences in the big woods, the morality based upon them may be nothing more than a construct of his own consciousness. Just as the priestly ritual of the hunt fails to bring the hunters into harmony with the game they slay, so no ethical framework can ever hope to mitigate the blind human rapacity empowered by consciousness. Consciousness stands at the broken juncture between man and nature; conscience feels the guilt of separation but is unable to heal the breach.

Man's moral task in *Go Down, Moses* grows out of his religious quest; the human person must treat his fellows and fellow creatures with respect because only in this way can he make himself accessible to the spirit of nature. But as is true for the ritual of the hunt, the respect due to creatures who have their own dignity is incompatible with the assertion of will necessary for survival. Just as the only means to complete reunification with nature is death, so the only way to insure the integrity of the other is to deny one's will altogether. In both cases what is lacking is the middle ground of reconciliation which allows one to "slay" and love at the same time. Ike, the man of conscience, chooses not to kill; paradoxically, this choice leads in a sense to his death. He removes himself from the human society where the tragic necessity of self-assertion is accepted. But of course to make the other choice would be to accept the inevitable failure of morality. The will to power makes moral purity impossible in the ethical sphere just as consciousness frustrates union with nature in the religious.

The attempt to establish a solid basis for human morality in Faulkner's myth is doomed to failure, then, for two reasons. First, as in Ike's experience of the numinous in the big woods, there is always the nagging suspicion that honor and courage and love are nothing more than the artful contrivances of human consciousness. Boon's love tryst with Lion and Ben is certainly subject to the alternative explanation that what appear to be courage and love are in fact raw expressions of the will to power. In addition, there is built into the denial of the will to power an implicit rejection of life. To refuse to assert oneself at the expense of the other is to choose death. Human survival depends on a violation of nature and the other which is inherently immoral. Faulkner refuses to submit to the temptation of saying either that Ike is deluded, or that his attempt to conquer consciousness and the will to power may succeed. Faulkner's myth is therefore ironic, his vision tragic. Human dignity has its source in the willingness to hold values which may be illusions and to live by them while recognizing that the task is impossible.

What distinguishes *Go Down, Moses* as the highwater mark of Faulkner's fiction is his ability here to join the mythic and ironic modes of his art. His attempt to indict and escape the South has here been modified into a unified vision which gives him critical perspective on his native country. He is no longer paralyzed by the burden of his cultural heritage after the fashion of

Quentin Compson nor must he jettison history altogether in favor of the comforting illusions of pastoral artifice. In *Go Down, Moses* he is able to see the South as an instance of the larger tragedy of human existence. Faulkner has here made the moral choice of which his character Ike is incapable: to accept the tragic quality of life and the possibility of nihilism without giving way to despair.

CONCLUSION

The ironic myth of *Go Down, Moses* completes the enterprise which Faulkner began in *The Sound and the Fury*. Faulkner's first great work draws its power from the heroic attempt he makes through four narrators to overcome the chaos brought on by the collapse of a traditional system of values. The tragedy of Caddy, who is the silent center of the novel, is representative of a crisis in Southern culture: the virtues of a tradition symbolized in the ideal of the white woman now appear to be bankrupt. The four sections of the novel offer varying accounts of the crisis that has ensued, but each for different reasons is inadequate to explain it. The poles between which the four failed explanations fall are now, from the perspective of the ironic myth, clear. They are the spheres of myth and history.

For Jason, Caddy's downfall is simply the result of her own misguided response to circumstance, to the forces of heredity and environment. Quentin, on the other hand, prefers to interpret Caddy's fate in mythic terms. He attempts to seal himself and his sister in what he imagines as a private room in hell, where her actions are the repetition of universal patterns. Quentin longs, in other words, for the eternal "now" of myth, where human events repeat the endless cycle of nature and thus fall into an established pattern of meaning.

Benjy, unafflicted by the curse of consciousness, does indeed dwell entirely in the eternal now, in the eternal now of idiocy where the cyclical routines that Dilsey provides enable him to enjoy the bliss of mythic repetition which Quentin craves but cannot quite achieve.

Dilsey alone manages to reconcile myth with history. Though her unifying vision is one which Faulkner himself cannot fully share, it offers the one glimpse of hope to be found in the novel. For Dilsey the demise of the Compson family is at once the result of their own freely chosen destiny and part of the larger mythic drama of human sin and salvation. And her pronouncement after the Rev. Shegog's Easter sermon, that she has seen the first and the last, has a double meaning. For she has seen the beginning and the end of the Compson household, but she has also seen the Alpha and Omega in the light of that *Heilsgeschicte* which is posited by the Christian gospel.

Time is meaningful for Dilsey not because it has been annulled in the eternity for which Quentin longs but because the ticking away of historical time, which represents the flow of life, though it cannot be halted, is yet redeemable by agape. And she keeps accurate time by her inaccurate clock because the hours of her days are ordered by her Christian faith.

A further sign of Dilsey's triumph is her harmonious relationship with nature. For Quentin, nature is the enemy which he can never conquer, and his suicide signalizes his final defeat by nature as well as history. Jason also sees nature as an enemy, but as one which the will may vanquish. Cotton crops, sex, and finally the Compson land itself are commodities which have meaning only in the economic nexus. Jason is content with his estrangement from nature, and he lives a sterile and lonely life as a result. Benjy never falls into knowledge and therefore never experiences estrangement from nature. Only Dilsey is able to acknowledge her separation from nature and yet live at peace with it. In the image with which the final section of *The Sound and the Fury* begins, she rises out of the morning mist, at one with the slowly awakening earth. She is both a distinctly human creature and one who fits perfectly the contours of the natural world. Nature, like time, is her home but not her prison.

Faulkner thus seems to extol Dilsey as a character who has achieved a reconciliation of myth and history which not even Ike McCaslin is able to accomplish. She appears to represent, here in his first great work, the victorious resolution of the struggle which empowers all his fiction. Yet, though he extols Dilsey's virtues, Faulkner appears to view with some scepticism the Christian belief which undergirds those virtues. The metaphors of theatricality and artifice which he employs in describing the Easter service suggest that Dilsey's religious vision may be the product of a masterfully-staged illusion.

The Rev. Shegog is presented as a virtuoso of appearances. His sermon is an adroitly executed rhetorical exercise which anticipates Faulkner's own ironic myth. Just as Faulkner's art is poised between myth and history, so Shegog is compared to a tight-rope walker who is balanced on the wire of his voice between the white and black worlds whose dialects he alternately employs. And when his sermon reaches the climax which elicits Dilsey's declaration of faith, the novel appears to be suggesting that the resurrection being celebrated may be only a mirage.

Faulkner is aware as Dilsey is not that the mythic framework which makes her faith possible may, after all, be a fiction. His attitude toward Dilsey's Christianity is thus ambivalent. While he admires her goodness, he is unable to give his suffrage to the faith on which her life is grounded. Dilsey is presented, in other words, as a kind of primitive. She is able to overcome the curse of consciousness largely because she does not bear its full weight; and Faulkner is only willing to entertain her Christianity as an aesthetic possibility. Like Sam Fathers, she is the member of an old race that has never completely severed its ties with nature and myth. But the Compsons are accountable to and for a complex social heritage, and thus the religious faith of a Dilsey does not, in its simplicity, represent any sort of live option for them. Dilsey's religious vision, in short, is an atavism of primitive consciousness that does not present a norm under the judgment of which the Compsons may be declared to stand.

From the perspective of the ironic myth of *Go Down, Moses* we can see why it is that Faulkner in his first great work has used "a doomed girl with muddy drawers" to epitomize the crisis of Southern culture. The South, like old Uncle Ike asleep in his tent, has had its falsely innocent slumbers disturbed by the disorders of history; the romance with which it has insulated itself is breaking apart. As Quentin correctly sees, the romance of innocence cannot admit the legitimacy of female sexual desire and survive. Caddy's unapologetic sexuality in *The Sound and the Fury* is therefore a symbol of the historicity which Southern culture has long denied.

For Faulkner, sex inevitably plunges man into history. It is at once an undeniable animal passion which will not allow man to escape his origins in nature, as it is also the element in his life that makes him most aware of himself as a separate being, a creature of consciousness. The South's ideal of the white woman as a chaste vessel of virtue is self-deluding not simply because it gives a false image of women, but also because, in denying the sexuality of white women, it denies history. Thus, like the daughter of Tennie's Jim in "Delta Autumn," Caddy represents not only a female sexuality which can no longer be repressed, but more importantly the encounter with history which the South can no longer postpone.

Faulkner turns to the South's particular history in *Absalom, Absalom*. Here he focuses upon the idea of the founding father, the second great cornerstone of the Southern romance. The story of Thomas Sutpen, as it is pieced together by Quentin and the other narrators of *Absalom, Absalom!*, reveals that at its core the South's understanding of its beginnings is naive. Sutpen insists that, in repudiating a wife and son and in using the threat of incest to force one son to kill the other, he has simply followed the logic of the social code that orders Southern society. The terrifying truth which emerges from the novel is that he is right. The Southern order, sustained by the illusion that it was created by blooded European aristocrats as the last bastion of genteel Western civilization, in reality was forged by men like Thomas Sutpen who aped the manners of the English country gentry as a legitimating mask. The code of honor and the trappings of refinement which the South has adopted disguise a ruthless grab for power. Sutpen is, as Miss Rosa says, a demon, but only because he has taken the romance of innocence at face value and so unwittingly exposed it as a deception.

Though he is not able to articulate it, Quentin has learned the lesson that Ike will make explicit in *Go Down, Moses*. The South's code of manners, its economic system, and, above all, its system of racial etiquette are based on no other value than the desire of the oligarchy to gain and maintain power. But so blinded has it been by its own myths that it has been unable truly to understand the logic of exploitation by which it actually lives.

The one point of ethical leverage within the Southern tradition is provided by its Puritanism. In the tale of Sutpen this voice is heard in the persons of Goodhue Coldfield and Henry Sutpen. Coldfield refuses to support the South in the Civil War because the purpose of the war is to defend an economic system built on "opportunism and brigandage." Though his critique of the Southern cause is certainly limited, he sees its presuppositions are immoral, and withdraws from it on the basis of ethical principle. His grandson likewise performs an act of repudiation when he kills his brother and flees his home in order to prevent the incestuous union of Charles Bon and Judith Sutpen. In this gesture which recalls Quentin's suicide and anticipates Ike's rejection of his patrimony, Henry seizes one horn of a moral dilemma. He has been forced by the dynamics of family relationships to choose between sustaining his family at the price of degradation and destroying his family in the name of morality. This of course is the same dilemma which faces Quentin and Ike. Quentin is finally unable to perform the act of incest which will preserve the unity of the family circle and, paradoxically, Caddy's "honor"; by committing suicide he effectively ends the Compson line. Similarly, in refusing to sanction the sins of his fathers by inheriting the profits of their exploitation, Ike chooses isolation and childlessness.

Sex and history are thus entwined in Faulkner's treatment of the myth of the founder, as they are in his critique of the ideal of the white woman. The romance of innocence is shattered for Henry Sutpen by a vicarious encounter with sexuality. Faced with the threat of incest, Henry forsakes the myth to enter history and, like Quentin but unlike Ike, is immediately undone.

Henry's reliance on the resources of "Coldfield morality" to repudiate Sutpen's design indicates that the myth of Southern history is also a religious myth. Behind the strictures of Goodhue Coldfield and his daughter Rosa stands the belief that the exploitation which marks the society built by men like Sutpen is a violation of the divine charter which sponsored the transformation of virgin land into a civilization. In Miss Rosa's estimation Southern culture as a whole has suffered divine retribution for the sins of a few demons such as her brother-in-law. The righteous many, of whom she counts herself one, may remove the Sutpen curse and thus preserve the Southern romance. In Faulkner's view, however, the Puritan morality which Miss Rosa would impose upon the South and to which Henry has recourse in his repudiation of his Sutpen heritage is itself an element in the false myth the South has perpetuated.

The enlightened aristocrat whose dark house is the moral center of *Light in August* tries to combine the myth of the Cavalier with Puritan religion in the same fashion as does Miss Rosa. She flees in outrage from the demon who suggests intercourse before marriage, and then becomes a recluse who writes heroic verse praising the gallantry of Southern warriors. After Gail Hightower is forsaken by a wife who flees in search of sexual fulfillment, he demonically clings to the pulpit from which he can preach sermons recreating his grandfather's daring cavalry escapade during the Civil War. *Light in August* explores the Puritan religion which is thus uneasily joined to the Cavalier romance in the minds of Rosa and Hightower. Despite the tension between the two made evident by the protest of Coldfield morality against Sutpen's design, Faulkner shows in *Light in August* that they are simply mirror images of each other. Puritanism is the religious twin of Sutpen's code. Not only does Sutpen represent the reality of the Cavalier type rather than, as Rosa thinks, a deviation from it, but the religious assumptions in terms of which she condemns Sutpen are revealed in *Light in August* to be themselves a mask for the will to power.

Faulkner's examination of Puritanism in *Light in August* shows it to be a code conceived without full historical consciousness, a flaw it shares with the Southern romance. Puritanism assigns to the individual responsibility to act out his salvation or damnation, and so it would seem that for the Puritan the world is a blank page on which the will writes its fate. At the same time, however, Puritanism represents the human will as utterly inefficacious in relation to divine predestination, since God's eternal decrees order human action and prevent man's entry into the freedom of history. Accordingly, Faulkner's Puritan characters are, in a strange way, equally willful and fated. Joe Christmas, who cannot escape the Puritanism against which he rebels, murders the woman who symbolizes the religious subjugation under which he has lived; but, in so doing, he feels that he is acting out the preordained pattern of his damnation.

The Puritan who would be saved must prove to himself and his neighbors that, though born a sinner, he has been regenerated and is on a pathway towards heaven. The evidence of his election is a godly life that, in McEachern's words, shows hatred of sin and love of work. While the ethic is different from that of the Cavalier, the importance of one's public life is essentially the same for both Sutpen and McEachern: the gentleman and the saint must both acquire those trappings which are signs that they have been "born" into the class of the elect. Thus the doctrine of election is the romance of innocence dressed in Puritan guise.

The Puritan, like the Cavalier, is marked by his disposition toward obsession and fantasy. Sutpen's single-minded devotion to his plan makes him oblivious to any other claim. His obsession runs to fantasy when near the end of his life, he clings to the dream of turning Sutpen's Hundred into a showplace of aristocratic refinement and seduces a white-trash teenager in the quixotic hope of producing the genteel son who will continue his line. And the Puritans of *Light in August* likewise become so obsessed with acting out their salvation or damnation that they are enmeshed in a fantasy which is completely divorced from reality. Doc Hines, McEachern, Joanna Burden, Joe Christmas, and Gail Hightower all repeat this pattern. Hightower, the Puritan preacher, acts as a bridge here, for his fantasy springs not from seeing himself as God's avenging angel, but from his identification with the Cavalier grandfather who was killed while raiding a chicken coop. Both Puritan and Cavalier are thus bent on forcing nature and history into the molds of their myth; they become entirely creatures of will and fantasy.

The result of the Puritan's obsession with will is that his religion becomes, as Hightower sees, a cult of death. The Puritan cannot afford any transaction with nature or with his human neighbor which would jeopardize the successful completion of his plan. As is the case with Sutpen, his devotion to his design prohibits him from experiencing love or any other extreme of "catastrophe or pleasure." The absolute reliance on the power of the rational will to achieve its end locks the Puritan into a prison of consciousness from which death brings the only release.

Joe Christmas is thus not only the victim of this religion of death but also its saint. His alienation from the natural world, his insistence on asserting the independence of his will from any force that would bind it, and his final acceptance of the end that seems to have been predestined for him are all marks of the Puritanism against which he seemingly rebels.

Like that of all Faulkner's characters, Christmas's alienation is symbolized in sexual encounters. Joe's first reactions to female sexuality recall Quentin's: he is angered and sickened. His discovery of menstruation plunges him into a disgust that is relieved only by violence. His adult sexual liaisons with white women typically end with his goading his lover into hatred by announcing that he is a Negro. Sex for him becomes a weapon with which he lashes out at the women who, no less than the men in his life, have attempted to subjugate him. The struggle with women reaches its climax in Joe's affair with Joanna Burden, who tries to force him to repent of his sexuality and to acknowledge his Negro blood, the sign of his less-than-human status. Joe Christmas is thus no exception to the rule that in Faulkner's fictional universe sex symbolizes the fall into history, the discovery of consciousness, and the exercise of the will to power.

The irony of Faulkner's treatment of Joe as a Christ figure, of course, is that Christmas has followed the course of damnation rather than salvation, but in the telling of Joe's story Faulkner has shown how the religion of the South is guilty of just this reversal. That is, what the Puritan takes to be the way of salvation actually produces the life of alienated damnation that Joe has led. As in the case of Sutpen, while Joe's actions appear to violate community standards they in fact accurately reflect the culture which has shaped him.

Faulkner deepens his critique of the religious element in the South's understanding of itself by contrasting Puritanism with the innocence of Lena Grove. Lena represents all that the Puritans are not: she is unselfconscious, above (or below) the stern morality of the community, in harmony with the natural world, and absorbed in her journey rather than its goal. As in the final section of *The Sound and the Fury,* Faulkner has focused on an earthy, primitive female figure to evoke the mythic consciousness that is not threatened by history.

The difference between Faulkner's treatment of Dilsey and his handling of Lena is that the latter figure shows no signs of having triumphed over history; for Lena history simply does not exist. And whereas Faulkner is not able to embrace Dilsey's faith except as an aesthetic possibility, his sympathetic portrayal of her as one who has seen "the first and the last" and is able, at least temporarily to bind up the Compson's wounds, suggests that she has achieved an ineffable wisdom. Lena, on the other hand, is pure innocence untouched by the besmirching hand of history.

Faulkner has in *Light in August* bifurcated myth and history; his ironic indictment of Puritanism is in no way qualified by the comic pastoral he places alongside it. Lena's story provides only a temporary escape from the grinding negativity of the tale of Joe Christmas. The false myth contained in Puritanism produces a religion of death in which the will to power is absolute but unacknowledged; it provides no protection from the terrors of history. The truly mythic world of Lena Grove is an illusion which historical man can enter only through the imagination.

In *Light in August* Faulkner has reached an impasse not unlike that of Gail Hightower. He faces an historical reality in which myths are only masks for the will to power and where the only alternative to history is fantasy. Hightower ends his final meditation on Joe Christmas with a retreat into the old reverie of his Cavalier grandfather; Faulkner leaves the story of Christmas for the pastoral of Byron and Lena. But in *Go Down, Moses,* the work which marks the completion of his vision of the relation between myth and history, Faulkner will return to the legacy of the Cavalier. And here he finds a way to unify myth and history.

Faulkner's strategy in the work written at the apex of his career is that of the ironic myth. The division that becomes clear in *Light in August* in the later book marks the distinct worlds of woods and town which make up Ike McCaslin's universe. But, here, Faulkner has crossed the border which was closed in the other works. Ike attempts to carry the values he has learned in the mythic realm of the woods into the historical reality of the plantation he stands to inherit. Ike is the first of Faulkner's characters to gain a critical perspective on the tradition for which he has inherited responsibility while also winning through to a mythic acceptance of nature.

Like Dilsey, Ike has learned to live in harmony with the rhythms of nature and of time. In an act of relinquishment which is beyond Quentin Compson, Ike is able to surrender the heirloom watch which represents mechanical time, to enter the *kairos*-time which Old Ben inhabits, and then to return to the sphere of history. But, unlike Dilsey, Ike possesses Quentin's acute awareness of history's terror. He feels the weight of the corrupt heritage which has been bequeathed him, and accepts responsibility for it. He also differs from Quentin and Hightower in that he is not paralyzed by history. Drawing on the resources of a myth which stands over against the Southern romance, Ike attempts to atone for the sins of his fathers by repudiating his patrimony.

The mythic understanding by which Ike lives is one that sees the possibility of a harmonious relationship between man and nature: human beings are equipped with the desire and power to slay, but, if that power is exercised with respect for the natural world that is thereby violated, the possibility of a communion with nature is preserved. In the ritual of the hunt which Ike comes to preside over as priest, slayer and slain are part of a brotherhood. The little society of hunters that forms yearly in the big woods is organized according to a hierarchy of skill and virtue rather than color and property. It therefore reflects the harmony of the natural order and gives the lie to the arbitrary social arrangements of the town. The hunters kill only according to the rules of the hunt which forbid the wanton destruction of tree or animal. The integrity of nature is in this way preserved, and the great stag and the legendary bear hover about the hunters as the incarnation of the spirit of nature with which man is here in touch.

It is this kind of mythic harmony which Ike attempts to reestablish in the town. He becomes aware of three great interrelated sins against the natural order which he believes have destroyed communion between man and nature in urban society. The first of these is the sin of property. In Ike's view, "dividing the earth into oblongs and squares" means making an object of that which has its own subjectivity. The kind of spiritual communion with nature that Ike has experienced in the big woods is impossible when the earth is, so to speak, drawn and quartered. The most grievous example of the sin of property is slavery, or, in its modern version, the racial caste system. Delving into the plantation ledgers, Ike finds in these chronicles of property a chilling story of human degradation. The black and white branches of his family have been locked in a mutually demeaning master-slave relationship. Most damning is the revelation that the property relationship has infected the most intimate human bonds, those established by sex and procreation. The founding father of the plantation, Old Carothers McCaslin, has not only used his slave's wife as his mistress, but has fathered a child on their daughter.

Once again, sex is the symbol of the inescapability of history, and incest is the sign of the South's refusal to confront history. Ike's discovery of his grandfather's sexual sins effectively destroys the romance of innocence. After reading the ledgers it is impossible for him to see the plantation his grandfather has built as a noble achievement. The real values which undergird town society are not those he sees in the big woods but the evil forces of power and lust. Like the sterling cup filled with gold coins which his uncle promises to bestow upon him upon his birth, the legacy into which Ike looks on reaching maturity has no more actual worth than that of a tin coffee pot filled with debts which the heir is obliged to discharge. Ike has been disabused of the lie which his fathers told themselves. But, unlike Faulkner's earlier enlightened aristocrats, he is not paralyzed by the bankruptcy of his tradition.

The last of the white McCaslins attempts to atone for the sins of his forebears by drawing on the lessons he has learned under his spiritual tutor, Sam Fathers. He searches for a means to reestablish the natural harmony which the will to power as expressed in the property relation has violated. In symbolic gestures which mirror his role in the hunt, he repudiates his patrimony and distributes money to the black McCaslins. But his efforts fail. The bulk of the property passes into the hands of Ike's white cousins, who run the plantation as it has always been run. The Negroes whom Ike has tried to compensate either become entrepreneurs themselves (witness Lucas Beauchamp) or fall victim to social mores which remain racist (the daughter of Tennie's Jim and the grandson of Lucas and Molly are such victims.) Ike has confronted history from the perspective of the new myth of the big woods, but he has been unable to overcome the alienation which infects it.

From Faulkner's own vantage point, Ike has misread the myth of the hunt. In the episode which provides the climax of Ike's own experience in the big woods, the killing of Old Ben, Faulkner has left clear signs that man's alienation is an inherent feature of his existence, and that there is no mythic escape from it. The bear dies in the grip of a dog and of a man who are entirely consumed with the lust to kill. Sex and death are inextricably bound in the passionate tryst where Boon mounts the bear to save the dog with whom he has slept but cannot master. And "The Bear" ends with this same animal-like Boon shouting in a rage of frustrated greed over his thwarted attempt to kill the squirrels he has treed, as the logging train which is slowly destroying the big woods winds its way ever deeper into the heart of the forest.

Ike is unable to see that the will to power which infects society is inherent in the human condition; his vision of mythic wholeness depends on a denial of man's full historicity. The most telling evidence of this denial is the exclusion of sex from Ike's Eden.

Ike's own brief encounter with sex in his town life is symptomatic of his error. Ike's wife makes intercourse with him dependent on his claiming the plantation which is his by right. Faulkner knows, as Ike does not, that sex ushers human persons into an historical reality where the will to power is inescapable. By refusing to regard the earth as property, Ike has declined to embroil himself in the inevitable sinfulness of history, but he has also cut himself off from the flow of human life. The "power to slay" must be exercised if society is to endure in any form. Ike's wife forces him to accept the consequence of his refusal to impose his own will upon the world: he must withdraw from the on-going process of history altogether and so remain childless.

Ike lacks Faulkner's awareness that, given the inescapability of human history, the myth of the woods can only be an ironic myth. Human beings are condemned to history. The fact of consciousness means that man is alienated from nature by the very act of perceiving himself as autonomous. Perfect communion with nature is impossible unless consciousness itself is dissolved. Along with consciousness comes the will to power, the desire to master the world which one sees as object. The symbol that is present in Faulkner's ironic myth, but lacking in Ike's romantic myth, is sexuality. In sex the otherness of the partner and the desire to take something that one lacks are undeniable.

During Ike's single attempt, near the end of his life, to include sexuality in his romantic myth, he describes lovers as reaching a moment of perfect spiritual union in which they become God. Faulkner has the guilt-ridden Roth Edmonds reply that, if Ike is right, "then there are some Gods in this world I wouldn't want to touch, and with a damn long stick" (348). Here we see the note of irony that is present in Faulkner's myth but absent in Ike's. In the death struggle between Ben, Lion, and Boon Ike sees only ritual union; Faulkner knows that it is also an image of the will to power in human history.

But Faulkner does not undermine the myth altogether. For him, something like a limited reconciliation between history and myth is possible. Although like the appearances of the great stag in "The Old People" moments of hierophantic epiphany are rare and always subject to doubt, they come to some of those who wait with "patience and humility." While truth and honor and humility and endurance remain subject to subversion in the sinfulness of history, Faulkner refuses to believe that they are the products of fantasy.

In *Go Down, Moses,* the human enterprise emerges as tragic but not hopeless. The man of conscience is, like Isaac McCaslin, doomed to fail in his attempt to overcome the alienation of history, but this failure is itself noble and pregnant with meaning. While the mythic patterns in which he places his trust are always subject to doubt, they need not be the blind deceptions of the romance of innocence. Alienated man may not withdraw into a realm of mythic purity, but he need not resign himself to an amoral historicity.

Through the ironic myth which he finally formulates in *Go Down Moses*, Faulkner come from the brink of nihilism to a tragic vision of human existence. In so doing, he has also found a way to shake the foundations of the crumbling cultural edifice into which he was born without burying himself in the resulting rubble. Like Ike, Faulkner is no longer paralyzed by the discovery of history; but, unlike his idealistic character, he knows that to enter history is to exercise the will to power, and thus to repeat in some form the sins of the fathers.

Faulkner's act of assertion was the creation of his "apocryphal country." While the ironic myth which is the culmination of his thought fails to achieve the unqualified religious affirmation he sought through art, it nonetheless transcends the terms of indictment and escape with which he began. In the works which he liked to call "noble failures" he found his own means to confront the tragic reality of history.

DATE DUE

APR 0 5			
DEC 2000			
APR 2 8 2001			
APR 1 6 '02			
NOV 0 6 '02			
APR 2 8 '04			
MAY 1 2 04			
JAN 0 3 '05			
JAN 0 4 '07			
MAY 1 4 2007			
MAY 1 9 2008			
GAYLORD			PRINTED IN U.S.A.